Testimonials from Isabelle's public speaking coaching practice **English That Inspires**:

'Isabelle's deep understanding of language nuances and her tailored exercises allowed me to refine my accent in a way that feels natural and authentic. Thanks to her guidance, I now feel much more confident when speaking with clients, ensuring that my message is delivered clearly and effectively. (...) Beyond just accent improvement, Isabelle creates a supportive and engaging learning environment, making each session enjoyable and productive. I highly recommend her services to anyone looking to enhance their English communication skills, especially professionals who want to make a strong impression in client conversations. Thank you, Isabelle, for your dedication and expertise!' — **Henk**

'Isabelle helped me improve my self-confidence and self-expression during job interviews. After the first session, she motivated me positively, encouraging more eye contact with interviewers and enabling me to express myself comfortably. She supported me a lot during the process, helping to clear all the question marks in my head. I thank her for her support on this path. I am very lucky to have crossed paths with her. If you are looking for a good coach, I would definitely recommend her. It's not over yet, and I'm sure I'll have the opportunity to work with her again.' — **Dilan**

'I reached out to Isabelle to help me prepare for an important English-language scientific presentation to a large audience. I needed assistance with the flow of my story, crafting concise and clear English sentences, practicing repeatedly, and building my confidence. Isabelle's support was invaluable in helping me overcome my fear of being judged and to feel comfortable on stage. (...) I highly recommend Isabelle to anyone looking for practical, positive, and effective coaching for public speaking. Her expertise, dedication, and approach made a real difference in my presentation, and I'm incredibly grateful for her support.' — **Annemieke**

‘I loved getting clarity on my story and being able to fully be myself in the process with Isabelle. She really sees you and always has amazing feedback and edits to make things more tangible and be more on point. Writing your one story is an emotional project. We want to trust the ones who we share a new version or angle of our story with fully. Isabelle is the one for me, who I can trust and experience my stories with. Most valuable, I feel I created a great base for my signature stories, and confidence to be able to weave them naturally into any context.’ — **Taya**

‘Working with Isabelle gave me the confidence and clarity I needed during a crucial moment in my career. Her support helped me feel secure in myself while preparing for important international interviews. Isabelle has a grounded, insightful approach that brings out the best in you. I’m truly grateful for our work together and would highly recommend her to any individual or business looking to grow with purpose and authenticity.’ — **Mihaela**

‘I started working with Isabelle because I wanted to feel more confident in my day-to-day conversations in English. She is a thoughtful and structured teacher who genuinely cares about her students. Isabelle created a personalized roadmap with practical feedback and tips tailored to my needs. She has been a wonderful teacher and a great person to work with, flexible, supportive, and encouraging throughout. I learned a lot from her and I’m truly grateful for her guidance and feedback.’ — **Pooria**

‘Thanks to our sessions, I’ve gained noticeable confidence in speaking English. My colleagues and friends have also observed the improvement. I’ve learned to slow down and focus on the distinct sounds of English, rather than defaulting to Spanish pronunciation patterns. (...) I fully recommend Isabelle to anyone looking to enhance their English communication skills. Whether you're a professional, a non-native speaker, or someone preparing for a specific role, Isabelle’s approach is adaptable and effective.’ — **Adriana**

Finding Your English Voice

The Essential Public Speaking Guide for Non-Native Professionals

Isabelle van den Heuvel

Finding Your English Voice: *The Essential Public Speaking Guide for Non-Native Professionals*

All text in this book was written by Isabelle van den Heuvel. The book includes one AI-generated illustration (hand gestures in public speaking), which has been reviewed and provided with alternative text for accessibility.

First Edition

Published by Bridge Hill Press

ISBN (eBook): 978-90-835866-1-8
ISBN (Paperback): 978-90-835866-0-1
ISBN (Hardcover): 978-90-835866-3-2

Paperback and Hardcover printed in the country of purchase

Cover design by Olayemi Bolaji

To Martijn, whose love and encouragement have been my anchor, and to our children, who remind me every day why speaking up and putting yourself out there matters.

A quick note before we begin

This book is here to share ideas, insights, tips, and techniques I've learned through my work as a teacher and public speaking coach. It's designed to support your learning and confidence, but it isn't meant to replace professional help.

If you're dealing with significant anxiety, mental health concerns, or a medical condition, it's always best to speak with a qualified medical or mental health professional who can give you personalised advice.

Table of Contents

Why This Book

Private public speaking coaching can be incredibly powerful. Often, clients are surprised by how much progress they make in just a handful of sessions. Coaching offers something unique: immediate, personalised feedback focused entirely on you. It also keeps you motivated, which makes staying on track and seeing real improvement so much easier.

But not everyone has access to a skilled coach. Maybe you don't have the time, the budget, or someone nearby who truly understands the challenges of speaking in a second (or third!) language. That's why I wrote this book: to give you as much of that guidance and encouragement as possible. Think of it as your companion, a way to bridge the gap.

This book brings together what I've learned from years of working with people from different linguistic backgrounds. They all share the same goal — to find their voice in English and use it with confidence. Finding your voice isn't just about words; it's about discovering who you are and expressing that with clarity and authenticity. It's about contributing in meetings, speaking up in front of others, and sharing your ideas without constantly second-guessing yourself.

Realising that many others are on a similar path will help you feel more grounded — and less alone — as a speaker. It will also make you a more generous listener: someone who connects deeply, listens with empathy, and truly hears others when they find the courage to speak up.

But even with that realisation, public speaking in a language other than your own can feel daunting. There's so much to think about: speaking clearly, organising your ideas, telling your story in a way that holds people's attention, managing your nerves. It can feel like juggling five things at once... and trying to smile at the same time.

Think about learning to drive. At first, you had to focus on everything: the gears, the pedals, the mirrors, the traffic. It felt awkward and overwhelming, and maybe you even wondered if it would ever feel natural. But with time and practice, something shifted. Your brain quietly absorbed it all. Suddenly, there you were — driving along quite nicely without thinking about every single move.

Public speaking in another language is much the same. At first, it's clunky and nerve-racking. But with some solid techniques, steady practice, and a willingness to get it wrong before you get it right, it begins to click. Before long, you're not just getting by — you're connecting with people, sharing your ideas clearly, and even enjoying yourself (yes, really!).

Who Is This Book For?

This book isn't designed for complete beginners in English. Instead, it's for:

- **Professionals, academics, and entrepreneurs** who want to improve their presentation skills or work more confidently in English-speaking environments.
- **Job-seekers and career-changers** preparing for interviews, or stepping into English-speaking workplaces and wanting to feel capable and prepared.
- **Anyone held back by fear of public speaking in English**, whether it's stopping you from advancing in your career, business, or personal life.

If you see yourself in any of these descriptions — or if you simply want to feel calmer, clearer, and more confident when you speak English — you're in the right place.

Your Personal Why

There's a reason you picked up or downloaded this book. Maybe you already work in an international environment and sometimes struggle to express yourself clearly — whether in meetings, presentations, pitches, job interviews, or social gatherings. Perhaps listeners often ask you to repeat yourself, or you notice them straining to understand certain words.

It might be that you've avoided giving important presentations in English altogether, unintentionally holding yourself back from career opportunities. Or maybe you've been asked to speak at a special occasion and feel caught between not wanting to say no and worrying you're not ready to say yes. You might even have an interview coming up for a role you really, *really* want, and the stakes feel higher than ever.

If any of this sounds familiar, you're in good company. I've seen these exact challenges come up again and again — no matter where someone is from, what language they first learned, or what industry they work in. Smart, capable people often find themselves blocked by barriers that feel frustrating and discouraging.

The good news is that these barriers can be overcome. The very first step is to uncover your why: the deeper reason behind your desire to improve or excel. Are you aiming to feel more confident at work or in your business? Hoping to make a memorable impression at an important event? Or ready to open the door to new opportunities in your career or personal life?

Whatever your reason, keep it close. That personal 'why' will guide your practice and keep you going on days when progress feels slow. As you move through this book, you'll learn practical ways to speak with clarity and confidence. Just as importantly, you'll discover how to show up fully as yourself in English.

How to Use This Book

I've designed this book to be as practical and user-friendly as possible, so you can dip in and out and find exactly what you need, when you need it. Here's what you'll see inside:

- **Clear sections**: Each part of the book is structured so you can quickly spot the main takeaways.
- **In the Same Boat**: Scattered throughout the book are real-life stories drawn from my work with clients (with details changed for privacy). These stories highlight common challenges and breakthroughs, and remind you that you're not alone.
- **Food for Thought**: At the end of each chapter, you'll find reflection questions and prompts to help you apply what you've learned. **These are optional – the book will still work for you even if you never write anything down**.
- **Toolboxes at the back**: A collection of quick exercises and tips to boost your language and speaking skills whenever you need a fast refresh.

My aim is to act as your 'paper coach,' walking beside you as you absorb the material. Make this book your own: underline phrases that speak to you, jot notes in the margins, highlight the parts you want to revisit. Maybe you'll flip through it between meetings for a quick boost of inspiration. Maybe you'll find courage in the stories of others. Or maybe you'll use the practical tips to polish your next presentation. However you choose to use it, this book is here to give you encouragement, clarity, and tools you can return to again and again.

Remember, every confident speaker started somewhere – this is where you start.

In the Same Boat

Paul was a successful scientist who had managed to avoid giving presentations throughout his entire academic career. Though fluent in English – he'd worked with international colleagues for decades – public speaking always felt daunting.

Then, just before his retirement, he was invited to speak at a special event: a 30-minute presentation to an audience of 300 experts in his field. It was a huge honour, but also overwhelming. He had created countless slides and had plenty of ideas, but struggled to organise them. More than anything, he was terrified of addressing such a large, knowledgeable audience in a language other than his native tongue.

As we worked together, we uncovered something crucial about Paul's story. Like many people, he'd grown up in an environment where he felt he had nothing important to say. That belief lingered for decades, quietly holding him back. We explored his personal why: the deeper reason he'd agreed to this talk. After all, he could easily have retired quietly and avoided the stress altogether.

Paul's why was deeply personal. He wanted to put to rest the shame of having sidestepped presentations his entire career. More importantly, he wanted to share his life's work and contributions to his field. This was his moment to stand tall and claim the recognition he'd always deserved but had never sought.

For Paul, this presentation wasn't just about public speaking – it was about reclaiming his voice and taking pride in his achievements. The challenge was huge, but keeping his eye on that goal helped him stay motivated.

We could have worked on his accent, but that wasn't the priority. Instead, we focused on creating a compelling story and channelling his nerves into confidence. Developing his narrative and preparing him emotionally were the keys to unlocking his potential as a speaker.

I'll return to Paul's story in Chapter 2. For now, remember that no matter how intimidating the challenge, a clear and meaningful goal — your personal why — can give you the strength to persevere.

Food for Thought

1. Why have you sought — or are you seeking — work in an international environment?

→ *What draws you to cross-cultural or multilingual settings?*

→ *What does this setting allow you to become that perhaps a more local context wouldn't?*

→ *What values are you living out by stepping into a global space?*

____

____

____

____

2. Why do you want to become a good presenter in English? Is it about connection, career, confidence — or something else entirely?

→ *When you picture yourself presenting well in English, how do you feel?*

→ *What new doors might that open, professionally or personally?*

____

____

____

____

3. Think back to your most recent speaking opportunity: what made you say yes?

→ Was it a practical yes or a brave yes? Either way, what would you like to get out of this opportunity?

4. What are you most worried about? Is it pronunciation? The story? Your performance? Perhaps nerves?

→ Which of these worries do you tend to focus on most?

→ Are they rooted in something someone once said — or something you've assumed about yourself?

→ And what would it feel like to let go of one of those worries, even just a little?

5. One small thing I'll try this week to move forward:

Chapter 1: Tools for Creating Clear, Listener-Friendly Speech

1.1 Treasure Your Accent

Clients often ask me whether they should focus on getting rid of their accent. My answer to that is a resounding no. Your accent is part of who you are, part of your cultural and linguistic background and something you should embrace and be proud of.

On the whole, being bilingual or multilingual often gives you an advantage over monolingual English speakers in understanding other non-native English speakers. You have, after all, been exposed to a wide range of sounds, rhythms, and pronunciation patterns. This has sharpened your ear to subtle differences in speech, generally boosting your ability to understand various non-native English accents much more easily than monolingual English speakers can.

1.2 Listener Fatigue

That's not to say you shouldn't work on your accent to become a more listener-friendly speaker – in fact, you absolutely should. Let me illustrate why. A friend once shared an experience from a conference he attended. The main speaker, a Latin-American scientist with a Ph.D. in online security, had travelled to the Netherlands to present groundbreaking findings in his field of expertise.

Unfortunately, despite my friend having a good command of English, he couldn't understand a word of the presentation. He described the talk as 'one long unintelligible blur,' an incredible pity for both the speaker and the audience, especially given the importance of the topic.

Not only did this mean that the audience missed out on valuable insights, but it also likely left the speaker feeling frustrated and disheartened. To make matters worse, my friend added that the effort required to figure out the presentation was mentally exhausting. This caused his mind to wander and tune out. This phenomenon is called 'listener fatigue' and it's something every speaker wants to avoid.

This story highlights a crucial point: effective communication is about more than just speaking the right language — it's about making your message clear and engaging for your audience. Although accents are an important reflection of your heritage and identity, clarity is key when sharing important information or stories. Working on your pronunciation doesn't mean erasing your accent; it means fine-tuning it so others can connect with your ideas effortlessly. So, if you ever feel discouraged about refining your accent, remember that it's not about losing who you are; it's about ensuring your voice is heard, your message understood, and your audience informed and (hopefully) inspired.

1.3 Accent Bias

Before we dive into specific tools to adjust your pronunciation, let's address something important. That inner critic might tell you otherwise, but your accent is not 'a problem to be fixed.' So never, ever let anyone make you feel inferior because of your accent. Accents are a beautiful reflection of who we are — our history, culture, and identity. Sadly, some people believe their own accent is superior to others', but this couldn't be further from the truth.

Let me start by sharing a personal story. When I was seven years old, my family emigrated to New Zealand. I didn't speak a word of English at the time, and I remember being teased for my Dutch accent — kids would mimic me and laugh, which was tough to handle at that age. But children are incredibly adaptable, and within a year, I was speaking English better than Dutch.

Years later, as a young adult back in the Netherlands, I enrolled at university to study English language and literature. Feeling confident in my fluency, I applied for an exemption from the speaking classes. The final decision rested with the head of the English linguistics department — let's call him Professor Higgins — who spoke what's often referred to as the Queen's English (to put it simply: a very posh accent).

We had a perfectly pleasant conversation, and at the end of our meeting, Professor Higgins confirmed that I was indeed a native speaker and wouldn't need to attend speaking classes. 'But,' he added, 'would you please do your best to get rid of that *ugly* New Zealand accent?'

His words left me feeling embarrassed and self-conscious, as if there was something wrong with me. Believe it or not, I even apologised. For some months afterwards, I felt awkward presenting in front of my peers, afraid of being judged not for what I said but for how I sounded.

Thankfully, that changed when I confided in another professor, who kindly reassured me that Professor Higgins' remark was completely out of line. This professor reminded me that the Queen's English is just one variation of English — a minority accent, in fact. Realising that my accent was just as valid as any other helped me regain my confidence. Looking back now, I can see how absurd it was to feel inferior because of something as personal and unique as my accent. So, let me say it again:

Never, ever let anyone make you feel inferior because of your accent.

1.4 Techniques for Pronunciation Improvement

There are rarely quick fixes for anything worthwhile, and this includes accent enhancement. However, applying even one of the following techniques can do wonders for making your English easier to understand and for building your confidence as a speaker. Apply them all, and you'll be amazed at what you can achieve.

That said, please don't feel overwhelmed by the following sections. While these lessons are not exhaustive — entire books have been written about improving English pronunciation — **I have carefully selected only the most practical and impactful elements to include here**, things I've personally tried and tested. Even so, it's natural to feel like there's a lot to take in. So, focus on progress, not perfection. Remember, no matter your position or stage in life, you are a work in progress, and every step you take counts.

You'll notice that I've given the most attention to word and sentence stress. That's because they shape the natural rhythm of English, which is one of the most powerful tools for becoming a listener-friendly, confident speaker.

At the end of this chapter, I'll show you how to bring everything together and apply it to your own text — whether it's a talk, a pitch, or a presentation — so that your pronunciation supports your message and helps you sound more fluent and engaging. For now, simply treat the next few sections as practical tools. Working on even one can make a noticeable difference!

1.5 Pronunciation Through Sound Practice

One effective way to improve your English pronunciation is through **phonetic breakdown** — separating words into their individual sounds, or *phonemes*. This helps you focus on how each sound is produced, especially those that don't exist in your native language. Remember, it's not about sounding like a native speaker, it's about becoming a clear speaker who is easily understood.

You might now be wondering: *Which sounds should I focus on? Which words should I practise? And how do I even start?* The answer depends on your language background, but the **method** is the same, no matter where you're from.

A Simple Method for Clearer Pronunciation

Use this three-step practice routine to master any tricky sound in English:

1. **Word Practice**: Start with 5–10 common words that include the sound you want to work on. Underline or highlight the target sound so it stands out. Really concentrate on pronouncing the words properly by saying each one slowly and deliberately.
   Example: f**i**sh, d**i**sh, sh**i**p, s**i**ster, f**i**n**i**sh
2. **Sentence Practice**: Now use those words in short, simple sentences. Again, speak slowly and deliberately.
   Example: The f**i**sh **i**s **i**n the d**i**sh. / My s**i**ster likes to f**i**n**i**sh work early.
3. **Fluency Practice**: When the sound starts to feel more natural, move on to a short paragraph or dialogue that includes the target sound, along with similar sounds (to help you hear the difference). This helps reinforce what you've learned in real speech.

The key to success is **repetition**. Just a few minutes of daily practice can help you internalise the correct pronunciation until it becomes automatic. Now, let's look at two examples:

Example #1: Romance language speakers: the short /ɪ/ sound

Let's take the example I used above. It comes from speakers of Spanish, Portuguese, French, Italian, and Romanian, who often struggle with the tight, short English vowel sound /ɪ/, as in *fish, dish, sister, ship,* and *finish.* This subtle sound doesn't exist in all Romance languages, so it's often replaced with a longer vowel sound, leading to mispronunciations like:

- *feesh* instead of *fish*
- *sheep* instead of *ship*

- *seester* instead of *sister*
- *feeneesh* instead of *finish*

Often, this lack of correct distinction between sounds can cause confusion, as in the case of 'ship' and 'sheep.' I once heard a French politician consistently pronounce 'terrorism' as 'tourism' — no need to explain what kind of confusion that can lead to!

Using the three-step method:

1. **Word practice**: fish, d**i**sh, sh**i**p, s**i**ster, f**i**n**i**sh, **ini**t**i**al, s**i**x, r**i**sk, st**i**ck, d**i**scuss, l**i**st, q**ui**ck, **i**dent**ify**

   → **To make the sound**, keep your lips relaxed, your mouth slightly open, and your tongue high but slightly forward. Make the sound short and quick — like a tiny smile inside your mouth.

2. **Sentence practice**: The fish chased the sh**i**p. / My s**i**ster likes to f**i**n**i**sh work early.

3. **Fluency practice**:

   The **fish** swam **quick**ly past the **ship** and **hid** behind a **big dish** of seaweed. My **sis**ter tried to **finish** her sketch of **it**, but she **didn't sit still** for long. She **gig**gled when the **little fish did** a **flip**, then **picked** up her pen to **fix** the **image**.

   We had to **finish** the **initial** phase of the project by **six** o'clock. The **risk** was high, so the team held a **quick** meeting to **dis**cuss each **issue**. **Tim** created a check**list** to track progress and ident**i**fy gaps. With a **bit** of extra effort, we managed to **stick** to the schedule.

Example #2: Dutch speakers – final consonants and vowel shortening

Dutch speakers often harden final consonants when speaking English, which can shorten the vowel sound before it. For instance:

- *job* becomes *jop*
- *give* becomes *giff*

While this might not always cause confusion, it can sound jarring and unnatural to native speakers. It *can,* however, lead to misunderstandings in words that are minimal pairs (words that differ by just one sound), such as:

- *bed* vs. *bet*
- *bad* vs. *bat*

Using the three-step method:

1. **Word practice**: **job**, **give**, and distinguish between b**ed**/bet, b**ad**/bat, b**id**/bit, s**aid**/sat

   → To make the sound, prolong the vowel in **bold** and soften the final consonant – for example, 'b**ed**.'

   → Use short, crisp pronunciation with words ending in 't,' – for example, 'bet.'

2. **Sentence practice**: She ga**ve** me the **job**. / The b**ed** is r**ed**.

3. **Fluency practice**:

   I **said** the patient looked a bit tense this morning. His wife was worried and sat by his **bed** all night. I'll **give** him something for the pain he mentioned and check his chart. He told me he lost his **job** last week; I bet stress is making everything worse.

> In every **job**, HR needs to **give** people a fair chance. A **good** bet is that the best choice is not always the most **ob**vious one. A **bad** hire can hurt a team, but the right person can be a **big** win. What someone **said**, or how they sat in the interview, can show more than a strong **bid** to get the **job** or a bit of experience on paper. In the end, the right choice feels like hitting the bat at just the right time.

What You Can Do Now

Choose one sound this week that you know is tricky for you, or find one based on your native language background (if you can't think of one, check out **Toolbox 1** first). Then run it through the three-step method:

1. Practise it in individual words
2. Use it in clear, simple sentences
3. Reinforce it in short, fluent speech

Don't worry about sounding perfect, that's not the goal. Focus on being clear and consistent. Even working on just one or two sounds can have a significant impact on your overall clarity of speech.

> → *Curious about the pronunciation issues your language or language group tends to run into? Head over to* ***Toolbox 1****, where I've laid out the most common examples for you.*
>
> → *Those who'd like extra practice speaking with the front of their mouth, can try* ***Toolbox 2*** *as well.*

In the Same Boat

Nora is an ambitious young woman from Madrid, working in a competitive international business environment in the Netherlands. When she came to me, her primary goal was to improve her pronunciation skills. She had noticed that during meetings, she was becoming more reserved and speaking less. This wasn't because she lacked English grammar or vocabulary skills, nor because she lacked ideas or insights — far from it. Nora is naturally a sociable, talkative, and highly contributing person.

However, she found that people often struggled to understand her, and this led to moments of visible confusion. Over time, these experiences made her hesitant and withdrawn. When Nora realised that this hesitation was affecting both her social life and her career advancement opportunities, she decided to take action.

We began working on improving specific sounds that were challenging for her. One area we focused on was the vowel sound /ɪ/, which, as I mentioned earlier, is tricky for many Spanish speakers. Another particular hurdle was the 'ea' sound, as in the word *earth*, which Nora consistently pronounced as 'aarth,' making it difficult for others to understand. Since her work at the company involved environmentally friendly power solutions, *earth* was an important word for her to pronounce correctly. To help her master this word, I paired it with a similar-sounding word she could pronounce more easily. We practised saying:

birthday — earthday

By repeating these two words together, she gradually got comfortable with the correct pronunciation. Once she was confident, we dropped the 'day,' and what remained was the perfect pronunciation of *earth*. This small breakthrough made a big difference, as she could now say a previously challenging word with ease and confidence.

Sometimes, however, it is necessary to bend the rules to make communication smoother and more natural. One of the consonant sounds Nora struggled with was the *v* sound, specifically in the word *wolves*. This made certain English plurals, like *wolf* and *wolves,* especially difficult for her. No matter how much we practised, she continued to pronounce *wolves* as 'wolbes.'

As this continued to be frustrating, I suggested that she simply pronounce it as 'wolfs' in the future. While this isn't the grammatically correct plural, it would ensure that her meaning was clear, and more importantly, it would allow her to avoid stumbling over her words. After all, clear communication is the ultimate goal, and sometimes small compromises like this can boost both confidence and fluency.

Eventually, Nora reported feeling much more confident at work. She began speaking up more during meetings, contributing her valuable ideas, and engaging in discussions without the same hesitation she had felt before. A milestone moment for her was when she finally said yes to giving a presentation, a task she had previously avoided out of fear of being misunderstood.

This time, however, she found herself not only agreeing to it but actually looking forward to the opportunity, for which we prepared using the approach laid out in this book. It was a turning point that made her realise just how far she had come.

Nora's story highlights a valuable lesson for anyone learning to speak up in English: progress isn't about perfection. Instead, it's about finding practical solutions that work for you. Every step, no matter how small, is worth celebrating. Sometimes, it's those small victories — like mastering a tricky word, sharing an idea in a meeting, or saying yes to a challenge — that add up to big, transformative changes.

1.6 Word and Sentence Stress for Creating English Rhythm

Remember my friend's story about the online security expert whose speech sounded like 'one long unintelligible blur'? While the expert's content was undoubtedly insightful, his delivery made it hard to follow. He may have made word and sentence stress errors by emphasising the wrong syllables, which can confuse listeners. More importantly, his rhythm patterns most likely played a crucial role in making his speech difficult to understand.

How you choose to stress parts of a word is one of the most important elements in creating clear, listener-friendly speech — I cannot stress this enough (no pun intended!). Let me illustrate. Many Dutch speakers pronounce the word graffiti as GRA-fity (with the stress on the first syllable and without a hard 'f' sound), which native English speakers often interpret as 'gravity' due to the identical stress pattern (the correct stress pattern is gra-FFI-ti).

Is this a huge problem? Well, listeners can usually use context to figure it out — but, and this is crucial, while they're busy 'figuring it out', at least part of your message may be lost on them. As we discussed earlier, when you make your listeners work hard to understand you, they'll often disengage, become bored, or tune out entirely. This can have a significant impact on the effectiveness of your communication, presentation, or conversation. Worse, it might undermine your confidence and the incredible joy you could otherwise experience in sharing your ideas with others.

When it comes to word stress, it's helpful to know that incorrect stress placement is a very common issue among non-native speakers and something you can improve considerably with practice. Let's consider these two examples:

- For many Chinese and Japanese speakers, there's a tendency to stress the **first syllable** in a word like 'hotel' ('HO-tel'), when native speakers stress the **second syllable**: 'ho-TEL.' This subtle shift can cause confusion because 'HO-tel' might sound unnatural or unfamiliar to your listener.

- Similarly, speakers of Hindi often place equal stress on all syllables. For example, they may say the word 'computer' evenly as 'com-pu-ter,' or put the stress on the wrong syllable, as in 'com-pu-TER.' In both cases, all the vowel sounds are kept equally short. The native English stress pattern, on the other hand, **emphasises the middle syllable**: 'com-PU-ter.' This naturally lengthens and changes the middle vowel sound, so it comes out more like 'com-PYU-ter.'

To help you along, here is a list of typically stressed and unstressed words. Note that the CAPITALISED SYLLABLES indicate stressed parts of the words, and the *italicised* syllables at the end of a sentence indicate downward inflection ↘ , something we will explore more closely in 1.8. For now, it's enough to know that this means **going down at the end of the sentence**.

These stress and intonation patterns often depend on whether a word is a **content word** (carries meaning) or a **function word** (grammatical role, usually unstressed). **Function words are typically unstressed** and serve grammatical purposes. In the following examples, words in UPPER CASE are stressed (to emphasise their importance in the sentence), while lower case words are unstressed (since they serve more of a grammatical function):

- **Articles (the, a, an):**
  'The re-PORT is DUE TO-*day*.' ↘
  'I SENT a DRAFT this MOR-*ning*.' ↘

- **Auxiliary verbs (is, are, have, will):**
  'We're MEET-ing with the CLI-*ent*.' ↘
  'She has SENT the E-*mail*.' ↘

- **Prepositions (in, on, at, by, for):**
  'The FILE is on the SER-*ver*.' ↘
  'We'll MEET at the AIR-*port*.' ↘

- **Conjunctions (and, but, or, because):**
  'We need MORE TIME and MORE *STAFF.*' ↘
  'I TRIED to CALL but NO-one AN-*swered.*' ↘

- **Pronouns (he, she, it, they):**
  'He WORKS with our *TEAM.*' ↘
  'They WANT us to JOIN the *CALL.*' ↘

- **Determiners (this, that, my, your):**
  'This PRO-ject is UR-*gent.*' ↘
  'Your TEAM did a GREAT *JOB.*' ↘

- **Modals:** (expressing necessity, possibility, or permission – stress changes depending on what is emphasised)
  'We must sub-MIT the re-PORT by *noon.*' ↘
  'We MUST sub-mit the re-PORT by *NOON.*' ↘
  'You can FIN-ish the TASK to-MOR-*row.*' ↘
  'You CAN FIN-ish the TASK to-MOR-*row.*' ↘

- **Some adverbs:** (adverbs that aren't essential to the meaning of the sentence are often de-stressed)
  'She was really TI-red after the WORK-*shop.*' ↘
  'It's quite BU-sy to-*DAY.*' ↘

- <u>Note</u> that the word 'busy' is pronounced 'BI-zzy' (with a short, crisp /ɪ/ sound).

- **Some auxiliary phrases**: Words like 'do' and 'have' used in questions or negations are usually unstressed unless being emphasised:

- 'I DO like giving PRE-sen-TA-tions, you *know*!' ↘

- 'We HAVE to leave soon, or we'll be LATE for our a-PPOINT-*ment.*' ↘

Sentence stress and developing English rhythm are skills you can absolutely develop with practice. Start by listening closely to how native speakers emphasise certain words and 'de-stress' others. Try mimicking their patterns, perhaps by listening to short sentences and repeating them out loud. For example, take a sentence such as:

'**What are you doing tomorrow**?'

Notice how it sounds more like:

'**What're-you DO-ing to-MOR-row**?'

The words '**What are you**' are reduced to '**What're-you**' (almost like '**wateryou**'), while parts of 'DO-ing' and 'to-MOR-row' are stressed.

Once again — and you'll hear me say this often — don't be discouraged if your rhythm feels off right now. Progress takes time, and every small step you take adds up to big strides in the end. Whenever you find yourself becoming critical or impatient with yourself, just repeat out loud this beautiful affirmation I came across many years ago. Here it is with the correct rhythm:

NA-ture never RUSH-es its WORK, and I am a PART of NA-*ture* ↘

1.7 Intonation and Pitch

First, let's clarify what intonation and pitch are, and how they are related:

- **Pitch** refers to the frequency of sound in your voice, determining how high or low it is.
- **Intonation** is the variation in pitch throughout your speech, used to emphasise meaning or express emotion.

In simpler terms, **intonation is the *melody* of your speech**; it's how your voice rises and falls (i.e., pitch changes), not just within a single sentence but across your presentation or talk as a whole.

A flat, monotone delivery can make even the most motivated listener lose interest and make your message difficult to follow, as we saw earlier with the online security expert. By contrast, effective intonation — variations in pitch — brings your words to life, making them clearer, more engaging, and easier to understand. Intonation is used for:

- **Highlighting key words in your speech**
  Think of intonation as a verbal highlighter. Use it to show your audience what's most important. For example:
  '*This discovery is **revolutionary** because it **changes everything**.*'

  By raising your voice slightly on 'revolutionary' and 'changes everything,' you make those words stand out, ensuring your audience pays attention to what really matters.

- **Showing enthusiasm and excitement**
  Imagine you're pitching an idea to your team:
  '*This strategy could **transform** how we **engage** with customers!*'
  If you let your pitch rise slightly on 'transform' and 'engage,' your excitement will shine through. This type of enthusiasm is contagious, and it will inspire confidence and energy in your listeners.

- **Expressing what you think about something**
  Intonation allows you to express your feelings about a subject — even when you're using the same words. Here's how the exact same sentence can have different meanings:

→ 'The film was **bril**-liant!' (with rising intonation) - You loved it.

→ 'The film was bril-liant.' (monotone delivery, with no variation in pitch) - You didn't like it, and your tone shows disinterest or sarcasm.

→ 'The film was **bril-liant**, but...?' (trailing off) - Objectively, the film was brilliant, but you're personally undecided about whether you liked it or not.

1.8 Upward and Downward Inflection

Upward and downward inflection are part of the broader concept of intonation. As we have seen, **intonation** refers to the overall rise and fall patterns in your speech. Inflection, on the other hand, focuses on the smaller, more specific changes in pitch that give strength, clarity, and nuance to individual words or phrases. It is vital for:

- **Signalling the end of a thought** (downward inflection)
  Example:
  'Our profits increased by 12%per last quar-*ter.*' ↘ — it sounds final, complete, like a statement.

- **Showing confidence** (downward inflection)
  Example: 'I'm certain this is the right strategy for the compa-*ny.*' ↘ — it sounds firm and assured.

- **Emphasising questions you might be asking yourself or your audience** (upward inflection)
  Example: 'What would happen if we launched this product next month?' ↗ — it sounds curious and inviting.

- **Keeping your audience engaged and your talk listener-friendly** (mainly downward and at the right moments upward inflection).

Example: 'We've reached an important milestone in our pro-*ject.* ↘ But where do we go from here?' ↗ — The shift keeps people listening.

Downward Inflection

Think of downward inflection, also called *falling intonation*, as the verbal equivalent of a full stop. It makes you sound decisive and sure of yourself and, as I mentioned above, signals the end of a thought. For example:

'Our results show a 25% increase in efficien-*cy*.' ↘

Dropping your voice slightly at the end of this sentence will project confidence and authority, making you sound convincing, credible, and like someone your listeners can trust and rely on.

As a non-native speaker, you may sometimes struggle with this. You might find yourself trailing off into quietness (I hear this often!), where the last part of your sentences is barely audible, making you sound unsure of yourself. Or, you might end sentences with an upward inflection — almost as if you're asking a question. For instance, a French speaker might say:

'Our results show a 25% increase in efficien-cy?' ↗

Here, upward inflection can unintentionally make your audience wonder if you believe your own statement! So, remember: **Practising downward inflection will help you sound more powerful and convincing**. It will leave no doubt in your listener's mind that what you are saying is true, dependable, and credible.

Upward Inflection

Upward inflection, also called *rising intonation*, is when your voice goes **up** at the end of a sentence. You've probably heard it in yes-or-no questions, like:

'Are there any questions about this strategy?' ↗

'Do you often wonder whether your English is easy to understand?' ↗

In English, we also use upward inflection to do a few other things, such as:

- To sound open or friendly
- To invite the other person to respond or comment
- To show that we're unsure or being polite

In everyday conversations, this little rise at the end is a way of saying: *I'm not finished yet* or *What do you think*?

Compare the following two sentences:

'This is our strate-*gy*.' (voice goes down ↘ — it sounds final, like a statement)

'This is our strategy?' (voice goes up ↗ — it becomes a question; you sound unsure, perhaps checking to see if you've understood what's being suggested)

Notice how the meaning shifts, even though the words are almost identical. In the first example, the downward inflection makes it sound like a clear, confident statement. You're telling your audience what the strategy is.

In the second example, the upward inflection turns the same sentence into a question. Suddenly, you sound uncertain, as if you're checking whether that really is the plan or asking for confirmation. This subtle change in tone can completely alter how your message is received.

Practice tip: Say both versions out loud. Exaggerate the rise and fall at first so you can really hear and feel the difference, then practise softening it until it feels natural.

→ *For practice improving your inflection, see* ***Toolbox 3***

Now, let's move on to another powerful (and somewhat easier!) tool: the pause.

1.9 Pause and Pace: Your Allies on Stage

All the people I've worked with tend to speak too fast, usually because of nerves and the strong desire to finish their presentation in English as quickly as possible. **It's completely natural to feel this way**.

However, rushing through your speech actually makes it harder for your audience to follow and absorb your message. It also takes away the enjoyment from delivering it — and it certainly doesn't help build confidence.

One of the easiest ways to slow down is to use the punctuation that's already in your text. Too often, I see people reading right past commas, dashes, semicolons, and colons. They're there for a reason: they make the text readable. And when you speak, they do even more — they tell you when to breathe, when to change pace, and when to signal that something important is coming.

- **Comma** (,) — A small pause. Enough to let your listener catch the meaning without breaking the flow.
- **Dash** (—) — A slightly longer pause, often adding a side thought or extra emphasis.
- **Semicolon** (;) — A link between two closely related ideas; think of it as a pause that's longer than a comma but shorter than a full stop.
- **Colon** (:) — A natural 'drumroll' in speech. It introduces or explains what follows, so pause a beat, then deliver the next

part as if you're unveiling something important. For example: *'They're there for a reason: they make the text readable.'* In speaking, you'd pause after 'reason,' then continue with a tone that makes the second part feel like the reveal.

Beyond punctuation, well-placed pauses are one of your greatest allies. A short pause between ideas or sections gives your audience the time they need to process what you're saying. It also gives you a moment to collect your thoughts, which helps you avoid rambling, stumbling, or trailing off. When used intentionally, a pause can add drama or emphasis, making your message more powerful and memorable.

How to Use the Pause

Here are a few practical ways to use pauses to your advantage:

- **Before key points**: Give a short pause before introducing important ideas. This signals to the audience that something important is coming, making them more likely to pay attention. For example: 'The solution to this problem... (pause) is simpler than you think.'
- **After key points**: Pausing after a key point gives the audience a moment to absorb it. It allows your message to settle in and helps make your speech more impactful. For example: 'This discovery changes everything.' (Pause for a few seconds.)
- **To control pace**: If you feel yourself speeding up, consciously insert pauses. This also helps regulate your breathing, which calms your nerves and makes you sound more confident and in control.
- **For emotional impact**: Pauses can help highlight emotion or thoughtfulness in your speech. By pausing, you give the audience time to feel the weight of your words. 'I will never forget the moment that we... (pause) discovered the solution.'

Now, let's look at how the pause can make or break a delivery. Here's an example **without pauses**, which doesn't work well:

'I know you're eager to hear the solution and I can tell you it's simpler than you think. In fact, it's a solution that's been there all along. The key is to think differently.'

Why it doesn't work well:

- The speech feels rushed, monotone, and the audience doesn't have time to process what's being said.
- The key points blend together, making them less impactful.
- There's no emotional space, so the message lacks the emphasis it deserves.

The result, one you'll want to avoid at all costs, is quite simply that the audience will tune out. And once they've tuned out, they're difficult to tune back in.

Now let's look at a version **with pauses** which, in combination with the punctuation, works well:

'I know you're eager to hear the solution... (pause) and I can tell you it's simpler than you think. In fact, it's a solution that's been there all along. The key... (pause) is to think differently.'

Why this does work well:

- The pauses help to build anticipation and emphasise key points.
- The audience is given time to absorb the message, which makes it more engaging and memorable.

The result, one you'll absolutely want, is that your audience will enjoy listening to you and be genuinely interested in what you have to say. This, in turn, will make *you* feel more confident, more at ease, and far more in control.

Pace: Speeding-up and Slow-ing. Down.

The pause and varying your pace are two of the simplest yet most effective tools you can use when speaking in public. These techniques allow you to control the rhythm of your delivery, highlight key points, and keep your audience engaged.

For example, imagine you're presenting a company's core values to a new team. To emphasise the importance of equality, you could say:

'Every human be-*ing*. Is E-*qual*.' ↘

or:

'Every. Human. Be-*ing*. Is. E-*qual*.' ↘

The deliberate pause after each word or phrase, marked by a full stop, makes your statement land with weight and clarity. This forces your audience to focus on each individual word, giving it greater power and ensuring the message resonates.

Alternatively, speeding up slightly before slowing down can convey excitement or urgency. For instance, in an academic conference:

'**We were racing against the clock, testing, adjusting, refining, and finally**...(pause) **we found**...(pause) **the solution**.'

Here, the faster pace mirrors the intensity of the process, drawing your listeners into the story. The end of the sentence slows down and pauses for impact.

Keep in mind that pausing allows you to regain control if nerves cause you to rush. It can give you time to breathe, gather your thoughts, and look confident — even if you're feeling anything but. For example, if you're answering a difficult question in a Q&A session, a deliberate pause before responding shows composure and control. You could say: 'That's an excellent question.'... (pause) 'Let me explain how this applies to our findings.'

1.10: Repetition: Your Other Ally

Repetition is a powerful tool in public speaking, yet often underestimated. By repeating key words or phrases, you reinforce your message and help it resonate with your audience. It's not just about saying something multiple times, but about using repetition purposefully to emphasise what truly matters. Just watch your favourite stand-up comedian: they understand like no other how repetition can drive a point home. The same goes for skilled speakers in parliament, places like the United Nations, or persuasive lawyers in court.

In your case, if you're presenting a key takeaway to your team, repeating a core value can make it stick.

'**Our goal is clear**: **we will grow**. **We will innovate**. **We will succeed**.'

Notice how the repetition of the words 'we will' builds momentum and emphasis. It's like a rhythmic chant that resonates with your listeners, giving weight to each word and making your vision unforgettable.

Repetition also adds a natural cadence to your delivery. When done with intention, repeating a phrase can keep your audience engaged and focused, giving them the opportunity to absorb and internalise the message. For example, when discussing the importance of teamwork:

'**Teamwork is everything**. **Teamwork drives innovation**. **Teamwork leads to success**.'

The repetition here ties everything back to the central theme of the speech (the importance of teamwork) and ensures the idea sticks.

However, don't overdo it. Repetition should feel natural and purposeful, not like a broken record. You want your key points to land, not to become monotonous. The trick is to repeat strategically — emphasising the right words at the right moments, without overwhelming your listeners.

In Q&A sessions or when dealing with complex ideas, repetition can help simplify and clarify your message. For example, in response to a challenging question, you could say:

'What we're really focusing on here is data. Data. And more data.'

This reinforces the point, guiding your audience back to the core of the discussion and making sure they leave with a clear understanding of your focus. Will discuss Q&A sessions in detail in Chapter 5.

1.11 Ways to Practise

Working on pronunciation and verbal delivery skills might feel tricky at first, but with a little practice, they'll soon become second nature. In the following sections, you'll find some simple and effective ways to get started.

Mirror Practice

One of the most effective exercises for improving clarity is mirror practice. Stand in front of a mirror and talk about a topic you're familiar with for a few minutes. To get into your English-speaking mindset, you could start by reading some of the sentences in Toolbox 3; these sentences contain the correct word and sentence stress. Speak slowly and deliberately, paying close attention to how your mouth moves and the sounds you produce. Focus on using the front of your mouth — this is how native speakers typically articulate their words.

Once you've done that, repeat the exercise, this time speaking freely about a familiar topic for a few minutes. Take a few minutes to think about what you're going to say, or even write it out. Again, speak slowly and deliberately, using the front of your mouth.

This exercise allows you to observe your speech patterns visually and make any necessary adjustments. Emphasise the stressed parts of the words by saying them slightly louder. Don't be afraid to exaggerate at first; no one else is listening (or watching!). Over time, this will help rewire your brain and build new habits.

Record Yourself

Read a short paragraph out loud and record it. Start with audio only; we will deal with video in Chapter 3, when we move on to performance skills. By focusing solely on pronunciation, you won't be distracted by how you look or how you come across visually.

Listen carefully to the recording and pay close attention to the musicality of your voice. Where does your voice rise naturally? Where does it fall? Do you sound flat or overly monotone? Do you tend to trail off at the end of sentences, as if unsure or apologising for speaking? These are subtle signals that your listeners pick up on, often more than the actual words you say. A voice that drops in energy or fades away can unintentionally suggest a lack of confidence or clarity, even if your content is excellent.

Luckily, these things are entirely changeable. By making small, intentional tweaks – such as slightly raising your pitch on important words, adding variety to your intonation, or simply finishing your sentences with more vocal presence using downward inflection – you'll immediately sound more confident, engaging, and easy to follow.

Keep in mind that this isn't about being theatrical or unnatural. It's about adding a touch more intention and warmth to how you sound, so that your message lands clearly and your audience stays with you. More importantly, as your delivery becomes more expressive and connected, you'll start to *feel* the difference. You'll sound more confident — and that, in turn, will help you *become* more confident. It's what we could call a virtuous circle: the clearer and more engaging you sound, the more you'll trust your voice. And so will everyone else.

Immerse Yourself

Immersion is incredibly important, but often overlooked. Surprisingly, even some of my non-native clients living in English-speaking countries miss out on this step by socialising only with people from their own language group — a missed opportunity to build fluency (and expand their horizons)!

If you don't have an English-speaking social circle, there are plenty of other ways to immerse yourself:

- **Watch** English-language films without subtitles (or with English subtitles if needed).
- **Listen** to podcasts or watch YouTube videos on topics you enjoy.
- **Stay consistent** by following a weekly talk show or TV series — or, even better, a daily one.

If you live in a city, consider joining an English-speaking Toastmasters group. It's a fantastic way to practise public speaking, connect with like-minded people, and learn in a supportive environment. If the idea feels intimidating, remember that everyone there shares the same struggles and is looking for a safe place to improve, just like you are.

Learn from Other Public Speakers

Another excellent way to improve how you use your English speaking voice is by studying speakers you admire: watch TED Talks, webinars, or interviews with experts in your field. Notice how they use their voice to make an impact and how they articulate using the front of their mouth. Imitating their style can be a helpful step towards finding your own English voice. Over time, you'll develop a speaking style that feels natural and authentic to you. After all, every great writer, artist — or speaker — starts by learning from others before discovering their own unique voice and style.

These techniques aren't about achieving 'perfection' (there's no such thing). The goal at all times is steady improvement. It's about ensuring your voice reflects the confidence, clarity, and enthusiasm that already exists within you. With consistent practice, you'll discover a unique speaking style that works for you, enabling you to connect much better with your listeners.

1.12 Marking Your Text

One of the most effective ways to improve your pronunciation, rhythm, and vocal delivery is to work with a prepared text. It could be a few paragraphs, a script, or even just bullet points that you want to bring to life.

Start by reading your text out loud. If possible, record yourself as you go. Listen back and make note of anything that sounds unclear, rushed, flat, or overly formal. Notice where your voice naturally rises or falls, and where it might need more variation or emphasis.

Then, take a pen or use digital markup tools to **mark the text**, helping guide your delivery. You can try:

- **Highlighting** the key words or phrases that carry the main message
- **Marking** natural pauses and underlining where your intonation should rise or fall
- **Adding** reminders for pronunciation — either using the phonetic alphabet if you're comfortable with it, or simply writing the word in a way that helps you say it correctly (e.g. *VEDG-ti-bols* for *vegetables*)

This process does more than just improve clarity — it builds confidence. You're no longer guessing where to breathe or when to pause. You have a ready-made map to hang on to. You can see exactly where to give weight to your message, and where to ease off. Let's look at how this can work in real life, using a case that's typical of the professionals I work with.

In the Same Boat

Juliette, a French sales specialist in her late forties, worked at a fast-paced international company where pressure is part of the daily routine. That constant stress began to take its toll, especially when she had to speak in meetings, where nerves often got the better of her.

At a certain point, Juliette's manager had told her that her sales pitches weren't convincing enough. Her French intonation sometimes made her difficult to understand, particularly due to her habit of using upward inflection at the end of sentences, making it sound as though she was questioning herself. Here is an example of what she would say:

'**This package costs 6,000 euros**...?' (rising tone, uncertain)

instead of:

'**This package costs 6,000 eu-*ros***.' (clear, confident)

On top of that, nerves made her rush through her speech, affecting clarity and listener engagement. To start making progress, we worked on breathing from the lower abdomen rather than the chest, helping her slow down and speak with more control. We also marked her text, incorporating:

- Correct sentence stress for natural English rhythm (capitalising stressed words within a sentence)
- Pauses to improve rhythm and flow
- Adapted spelling for tricky words

- Downward inflection to sound more confident and convincing
- Vocabulary corrections (e.g., biological vegetables → organic vegetables)

We also corrected word stress by capitalising tricky syllables. Here are a few examples, showing first how Juliette pronounced them, followed by the correct pronunciation:

- mee-DJA → **ME**-di-a (media)
- ve-ge-TAY-buls→ **VEDG**-ti-bols (vegetables)
- con-SE-quence → **CON**-se-quence (consequence)
- PO-liti-cal → po-**LI**-tical (political)

With these adjustments, Juliette sounded more confident, clear, and persuasive in her pitches. She no longer rushed, and her pronunciation made a lasting impact, eventually helping her win over clients with ease.

Example of How to Mark a Text

On the next page, you'll see how we marked Juliette's text. Please note that this is a completely fictional example — not her actual writing or any client's — though it reflects the kinds of stress issues she typically experienced. Some words we spelled phonetically to correct her pronunciation.

Try reading the text out loud slowly and deliberately to get a feel for how it sounds (notice the lovely sing-song quality of English you are now developing!). Of course, there are many ways to mark your text, so it's important to experiment and find the method that works best for you.

(Opening Pitch):

In to-DAY'S com-PE-ti-tive ME-di-a MAR-ket, con-SU-mer CHOI-ces are HEA-vily IN-flu*enced*. That's why we've de-SIGNED this ex-CLU-sive PACK-age to help BIZ-nisez like yours STAND OUT. (PAUSE)

For just 3,000 EU-*ros*, you'll get a fully CUSTOMISED CAM-PAIGN TAY-lored to HIGH-light the BEN-e-fits of your PRO-ducts and drive REAL en-GAGE-*ment*. (PAUSE)

(Industry Example and Call to Action):

Take the or-GAN-ic food IN-dus-try, for example. (PAUSE)

Sta-TIS-tics show a GROW-ing de-MAND for or-GAN-ic VEDG-ti-bols, and with the RIGHT MES-saging, you can po-SITION your brand as the TOP CHOICE. (PAUSE)

Our team uses data-driven rec-om-men-DAY-tions to en-SURE you get MEASUR-able re-SULTS, all while staying within industry best PRAC-tices and ob-TAIN-ing PROPER con-SENT for TAR-ge-ted OUT-*reach*. (PAUSE)

The CON-se-quence of not a-DAP-ting to market TRENDS? LO-sing po-TEN-tial CUS-tomers to com-PET-itors who are a-HEAD of the CURVE. (PAUSE)

But with OUR STRATE-*gy*, you'll feel em-POWER-ed, knowing your brand is in EX-pert HANDS. (PAUSE)

EVERY-thing is de-LIV-ered on TIME, with CLEAR re-PORT-ing on per-FOR-*mance*. If you're looking for a spe-CIF-ic a-PPROACH that guar-an-TEES IM-pact, let's dis-CUSS how we can ELEVATE your BRAND TO-DAY!

Food for Thought

1. What do you find most challenging when it comes to pronunciation?

→ *Is it certain consonants or vowel sounds that trip you up?*

→ *Do you struggle with word stress or placing the emphasis in the right place?*

→ *Do you speak quickly and find it hard to use natural pauses or varied intonation? As I mentioned in 1.9, I often find that non-native speakers skip over punctuation when reading out loud, especially the comma. But the comma is there for you to pause and bring a moment of rest in the sentence. Do you use it, or do you tend to read over it?*

____

____

____

____

2. If you're not sure, could you ask someone you trust for feedback?

→ *A teacher, a colleague, or a friend might notice something you don't.*

→ *Are there any patterns they've pointed out before? What did they say, and how did it make you feel?*

____

____

____

____

3. Start noticing and tracking your pronunciation habits.

→ *Keep a small notebook or a note on your phone.*

→ *What patterns do you observe?*

→ *Are there words or sounds that you consistently avoid — or overthink?*

____

____

____

____

4. One small pronunciation goal for this week:

→ *It could be as simple as slowing down, practising a tricky sound, or marking stress when preparing a text.*

____

____

____

____

Chapter 2: 'So, Tell Me a Good Story'

2.1 Using Stories to Build Connection

Whenever Harry, a long-time family friend, came to visit, he had a ritual. As soon as he'd stepped through the door, hung up his coat, and sat down with a big cup of tea, he'd say: 'So, tell me a good story.'

It wasn't just small talk. He genuinely wanted to hear something real, something that had made us laugh, think, or feel something that week. We'd each take turns, sharing moments from our lives. Nothing dramatic, necessarily; a conversation with someone, a moment of panic somewhere, something one of us had overheard on the bus.

Harry always managed to extract the best details with open-ended questions like 'What happened next?' or 'What did you say?' He knew instinctively that it's the little things — how someone raised an eyebrow, or the silence that followed a funny line — that brought a story to life.

One of the things I deeply enjoy is helping clients weave personal stories into their presentations, and whenever I do, I often think of Harry. Because at its heart, storytelling isn't just about keeping your audience entertained. It's about making a genuine connection, it's about moving people emotionally, it's about caring. Personal stories draw people in, make ideas stick, and gives your talk warmth and personality.

In this chapter, we'll explore how you can use stories, big or small, to create talks that not only inform, but truly resonate. Once you find the right story, your confidence grows, and suddenly your talk feels like something you can look forward to delivering.

2.2 Facts Inform, Stories Transform

Courses teaching you the art of storytelling are everywhere, and for good reason: storytelling is a powerful tool. Unlike simply delivering information, telling a story creates an emotional connection with your audience. When you're just sharing information, it can feel like you're talking *at* your audience. But when you tell a story, you're talking *with* them. A good story invites your listeners to bring their own experiences and imagination into the moment. Their minds automatically create images and feelings. They don't have to work to pay attention — the story draws them in naturally and effortlessly.

This is true for any speaker, in any context. But if English isn't your first language, storytelling can be especially supportive. It allows you to express complex ideas in a more human way: less technical and more emotional, which audiences find easier to connect with.

Let's say you're a business owner preparing to introduce a new product. Rather than listing off features, tell the story behind it:

- The late nights at your kitchen table
- The prototype that didn't work (and the one that finally did)
- The first time a client said, 'This is exactly what I needed'

That story doesn't just explain the product, it shows your persistence, creativity, and values. It's not just about what you made, it's about who you are, and that is what your audience connects with.

Think back to school. What do you remember best: a list of facts, or the stories behind them? For most of us, it's the stories. The reason is simple — stories give facts a shape, a face, and often, a bit of drama. They engage your emotions and imagination, which helps your brain hold onto the information.

Take Thomas Edison. You might not remember the year the lightbulb was invented, but you probably remember the story of him trying thousands of different materials before finding one that worked. The image of him surrounded by failed experiments is far more memorable than a technical explanation of filament resistance.

Or consider Alexander Fleming, the scientist who discovered penicillin. He left a petri dish out while he was away, and when he returned, mould had killed the bacteria in it. His colleagues often complained about how messy he was, but that 'mess' led to a discovery that would change medicine forever. That lucky accident — combined with his curiosity — became one of the greatest breakthroughs in medical history. Again, it's often not the chemistry we recall, but the story of the messy petri dish that led to a revolution.

Stories turn abstract ideas into mental pictures. They give facts a narrative structure — a beginning, middle, and end — which is how our brains are wired to process and recall information. Yet many people struggle with where to start and how to end. Sometimes they jump in too quickly or wrap things up without much impact, leaving their story hanging in mid-air. Unless it's experimental literature, every story needs a solid structure. Nothing fancy, just a clear beginning, middle, and end.

Why is this relevant to you? If you're not fully confident in your English, storytelling works tremendously in your favour. Speaking from personal experience makes your message feel natural — even when it's carefully prepared. You don't need to speak perfectly; you're sharing something real, shaped by a clear, listener-friendly structure. And when you add techniques from the previous chapter — like slowing down and pausing in the right places — your delivery becomes smoother, clearer, and more engaging.

2.3 Writing Relatable Stories

When you're putting together a story that really connects, start by thinking about the people you'll be speaking to. What is their cultural background? What are their experiences? What pressures or challenges do they face in their day-to-day work? If you can tap into that, your story will feel much more relevant and engaging.

For example, if you're speaking to a group of executives, it might really resonate if you share a personal experience, perhaps a tough moment in your career that taught you something valuable. Being open about your struggles, and sharing what you learnt from them, helps build a sense of empathy and trust. Your audience is far more likely to connect with you if they can see a bit of themselves in your story.

Start by setting the scene: give a bit of context so people know where you're coming from. Then, introduce the challenge or turning point — what went wrong, or what needed to change. Finally, share how things unfolded and what you took away from it. That final reflection is often the part that really sticks with people.

If you're a non-native English speaker, clarity becomes even more important. Keep in mind that it's absolutely fine to keep your language simple. In fact, that often makes a stronger impact than trying to use complicated words or technical terms. The goal is to be understood and to leave a lasting impression, not to sound like you've swallowed a dictionary. Here's an example of how to build a story:

Story Example #1

Let's say your topic is overcoming challenges, and you're speaking to a group of executives. Executives are no strangers to pressure, deadlines, or high-stakes decision-making. Here's how you might compose your story with the aim of really connecting.

→ **Start with a relatable opening, a specific moment in time**:

'It was late, past midnight, and I was still at the office, staring at the numbers in a financial report that simply didn't add up. The quarterly board meeting was the next morning, and the pressure was mounting. I'd run the models three times already, but something wasn't right. I remember thinking, If I can't sort this out by morning, I may have to answer some very difficult questions.'

That kind of scene — alone in the office, chasing answers under pressure — is something many senior leaders have lived through. It builds a human connection right from the get-go.

→ **Introduce the problem**:

Clearly lay out the obstacle you were facing, and why it mattered. For example:

'This wasn't just a reporting error, it pointed to a wider operational issue that could affect investor confidence. And the truth is, I started to doubt whether I'd caught it in time. I began questioning my own judgment, and wondering if I'd missed something obvious.'

This shows vulnerability without oversharing. It signals that even at a high level, self-doubt is part of the process, and that honesty builds trust.

→ **Describe the journey**:

Take your audience through how you handled the situation. Be specific. What steps did you take? What helped shift your mindset? For example:

'The next day, I did something I hadn't done enough of in those days: I picked up the phone. I spoke with someone in operations who gave me a completely different perspective. Together, we found the root of the problem was something hidden in the supply chain data that hadn't been flagged. I realised then how easy it is to get stuck in your own head, especially when you feel responsible for everything.'

This shows problem-solving *and* self-awareness. It also illustrates collaboration and humility — qualities that resonate well in executive circles.

→ **Reveal the resolution**:

Let the audience see how the story played out, and what you took away from the experience. For example:

'By the time I walked into the boardroom, I had answers, and more importantly, a clear action plan. What could've been a difficult conversation became an opportunity to show foresight and adaptability. That experience reminded me that leadership isn't about having all the answers — it's about knowing when to ask for help.'

This kind of resolution brings both relief and insight. It turns a high-pressure moment into a meaningful leadership lesson.

→ **Deliver the takeaway**:

End with a practical message that your audience can take with them. For example:

'So next time you find yourself under pressure, remember: asking for help isn't a sign of weakness, it's often the most effective way forward. The further up we go in our careers, the more we need to remember that we don't have to do it all alone.'

That final line reframes strength, which is often needed in executive culture — especially where vulnerability and asking for help are still sometimes seen as a risk or a weakness.

Story Example #2

Now imagine you're a university professor speaking to a group of students — people who know all too well the pressures of looming deadlines, academic expectations, and big decisions about their future.

→ **Start with a relatable opening, a specific moment in time**:

'It was 8 p.m., and I was sitting on the floor of my tiny flat, surrounded by crumpled papers and empty coffee cups. My laptop screen stared back at me with a blinking cursor, but I had no idea how to finish my final project. The deadline was twelve hours away, and failure wasn't an option. I was stuck.'

This opening draws the audience in by setting the scene with vivid imagery and tension. Many students will relate to the pressure of looming deadlines and the feeling of being stuck.

→ **Introduce the problem**:

Clearly define the challenge or obstacle you faced. This builds curiosity and keeps your audience invested. For example:

'This project wasn't just another grade; it was the key to my internship and, potentially, my career. But no matter how many ideas I brainstormed, none of them seemed good enough. I started doubting myself. Maybe I wasn't as capable as I thought.'

This creates emotional stakes and allows your audience to empathise with your struggle.

→ **Describe the journey or process**:

Share the steps you took to overcome the problem, highlighting any emotions, setbacks, or breakthroughs. For example:

'In desperation, I called a friend who'd faced a similar challenge. She told me something that changed my perspective: 'It doesn't have to be perfect; it just has to be progress.' I stopped trying to create the 'perfect' project and focused on finishing one section at a time. I also remembered to use the research I'd already done instead of starting from scratch.'

This shows growth and offers practical insights your audience can learn from.

→ **Reveal the resolution**:

Explain how the problem was resolved and tie it back to the bigger message of your talk. For example:

'By 7:30 a.m., I hit 'submit' on my project. It wasn't perfect, but it was complete. And to my surprise, the professor loved it — not because it was flawless, but because it was innovative. That moment taught me a powerful lesson: progress beats perfection every time.'

This provides closure and leaves the audience feeling both inspired and encouraged.

→ **Deliver the takeaway**:

End with a clear, relatable takeaway that ties your story back to your audience's lives. For example:

'So the next time you feel stuck, remember: focus on progress, not perfection. Whether it's a paper, a job application, or a personal goal, taking the first step is always more powerful than waiting for the perfect moment.'

This ensures your story resonates and provides a lesson your audience can apply immediately.

Remember that good storytelling doesn't need to be theatrical and dramatic, it just needs to be *authentic,* to be *you*. Start with a moment that matters to you and make it relevant to your audience. From that starting point, keep refining your delivery. Ask a coach or a trusted colleague for feedback. Watch how they respond — what lands, what doesn't. Every story you tell is a chance to build trust, show leadership, and connect on a human level. And in the world of business or academia, those connections often matter most.

→ *For tips on being mindful of different cultural norms, see* ***Toolbox 10***

2.4 Show Versus Tell

When used well, stories can reinforce your key message beautifully. They add colour and texture. They show, rather than tell. And they build your credibility — not because you're trying to impress, but because you're being honest, open, and human. Here are some examples that illustrate telling versus showing:

Show Versus Tell Example #1

→ **Telling (just the fact)**:

'Good preparation is key to a confident and successful presentation.'

→ **Showing (storytelling)**:

'A client of mine once told me she didn't have time to rehearse — she was just going to 'go with the flow'. She was bright, articulate, and knew her material inside out, but during the presentation, nerves

took over. Her mind went blank halfway through a key point. Afterwards, she said, 'I thought winging it would feel more natural, but I ended up sounding unsure of myself.' The next time, we worked together on scripting her opening, rehearsing her transitions, and practising out loud — again and again. When the day came, she walked into the room calm, clear, and completely in control. She later said, 'I thought rehearsing would make me stiff, but it actually made me sound like myself, just on a really good day."

Show Versus Tell Example #2

→ **Telling (just the fact)**:

'Even spontaneous speaking goes better when you've prepared for it in advance.'

→ **Showing (storytelling)**:

'One of my clients, an experienced engineer, was caught off guard when his manager asked him to 'just say a few words' at the end of a project wrap-up meeting. He panicked, mumbled something about how 'everyone had worked hard', and sat down wishing he'd said more. We talked about it afterwards, and he realised this sort of thing happened quite often: last-minute moments where people expect you to say something thoughtful, without warning. So, we worked on a simple structure he could keep in his back pocket: what was achieved, what was learnt, and a quick thank you. A few weeks later, it happened again. This time, he smiled, stood up, and said clearly: 'This project reminded us that cross-team collaboration really is our strength. We learnt a lot — especially about resilience — and I just want to say thank you to everyone who pulled together to make it work.' He told me later, 'It was short, but I felt like a leader. And I wouldn't have, if I hadn't prepared for the 'off the cuff' moment."

2.5 Balance is Key

Of course, a whole presentation can't be story after story; it's all about balance. Think of stories as seasoning: a little goes a long way, and the right amount makes everything more flavourful. Sometimes, your entire talk might revolve around one central story, with a clear arc that runs from beginning to end (just like Paul's — see 'In the Same Boat' on page 62).

Other times, it might make more sense to weave in a few shorter anecdotes to support your main points. There's no one-size-fits-all — what matters is that your stories feel relevant, human, and true to you. Used with care, they can turn an ordinary presentation into something genuinely memorable, and something you will look forward to delivering.

2.6 Keep It Simple

Please remember this incredibly important point, which will undoubtedly be a comfort to you and many others (my clients always look visibly relieved when I tell them this). When it comes to public speaking, one of the biggest secrets to success is simpler than you might think: using clear, straightforward language. It's one of the fastest ways to make sure your audience understands you and stays engaged.

This is not 'dumbing down' – it's creating clarity. And if there's one thing people love, it's clarity.

A lot of us think that sounding professional means using big, complex words and lots of jargon. But the opposite is actually true. Simple language helps your message land better, especially in high-pressure settings like meetings, boardrooms, or conferences.

I once worked with someone who put together a presentation full of complicated words because he wanted to sound fluent and polished. Unfortunately, it had the opposite effect – the text felt stiff and overly formal. On top of that, he struggled to pronounce some of the words, which made things even harder for his audience to follow.

One of the first things we did was simplify his script. For example, we changed:

'**We are endeavouring to enhance strategic alignment**.'

to:

'**We're working to get everyone moving in the same direction**.'

It made a huge difference. His message was easier to understand, he connected better with his team, and he got enthusiastic feedback. Down the line, those clearer, more engaging presentations even played a part in him getting a promotion.

Here's a quick tip: read your message out loud. If it sounds awkward or too formal, there's probably a simpler, more natural way to say it.

Of course, sometimes you can't avoid specialist words. But here's a comforting truth: even native speakers have words they stumble over. The word *anthropological* in English and *gediagnostiseerd* in Dutch still give me sweaty palms. And, believe it or not, if I'm not careful, I even trip over 'the Netherlands.'

One of my clients struggled with a word that gave her nightmares: *optimisation*. She couldn't avoid it – it was central to her work in online marketing. I taught her a simple technique: take a steady breath in just before the word, then say it on the out-breath. Slow down slightly, as if approaching a tricky roundabout, and break it into clear, manageable syllables. Let your breath guide you safely through the word.

Note that in the following example, I have added the correct syllable stress too:

'One of the most important ways to be found online is by ensuring **(begin to slow down here)** *your search engine* **(breathe in – and on the out-breath)** *op-ti-mi-SA-tion is set up correctly to attract your ideal audience.'*

It worked brilliantly for her; with a bit of practice, I'm sure it can for you too.

In the Same Boat

Remember Paul, the successful scientist I introduced to you in the opening of this book? The one who had spent his entire career avoiding presentations despite being fluent in English and respected in his field? When Paul was asked to speak at a major event just before his retirement, he was understandably overwhelmed. We worked together to put together a presentation that would resonate with his audience, transforming what could have been a dry, academic lecture into something much more engaging and personal. This is how we approached it...

Paul's upcoming presentation was a big deal: 30 minutes to a room full of experts, all keen to hear about the history of his groundbreaking research. But, despite being an expert in his field, Paul wasn't sure how to make his presentation stand out. He didn't want it to be just another dry, academic talk — those endless slides full of facts and figures that no one remembers. But at the same time, he wasn't sure how to change it. He knew he had the knowledge, but how could he present it in a way that would engage his audience?

That's when we began working together. Over a few sessions, we explored ways to breathe life into his presentation. We talked about storytelling, not just as a technique, but as a way for Paul to truly own his message. He didn't have to 'dress up' the content; instead, he could share his own personal journey through the research. His story was as essential to the findings as the data itself — and we were going to show the audience that.

One of the first things we did was step away from the slides. For sure they'd help him explain the research, but we needed to focus on the narrative. How could we build the story of his research in a way that resonated emotionally, as well as intellectually?

Paul started by sharing his own experience within the project; he'd been there for decades, after all. It wasn't just about the breakthroughs; it was about the people, the setbacks, the small victories. He told me, 'I want the audience to feel how hard it was, how much we fought to get where we are today.' And that's exactly what we worked into the presentation: the humanity behind the science.

Paul began to weave in anecdotes from his time in the lab, like the early days in the 1980s when their only tool was an enormous, antiquated computer that barely worked. 'We used to argue over who got to use it,' he said, 'as if it was the most prized possession we had.' He showed a picture of that computer, and immediately, the room felt lighter. His audience wasn't just hearing facts — they were getting a glimpse into the personal side of the research, the little moments that made it all worthwhile.

As we progressed, we uncovered another wonderful part of the story. The team's research had made headlines in the newspapers at the time; articles celebrating their success. Paul clicked to a slide showing those articles. 'This,' he said, 'was the recognition we'd worked so hard for.' The audience absorbed those moments of triumph with him, the small victories that are often left out of a typical academic presentation.

By the end, Paul's presentation wasn't just a talk about research; it was a story about perseverance, discovery, and passion. It wasn't dry or academic — it was compelling and human. And that was exactly what he had wanted all along.

In the process of working together, we didn't just rework his slides or tweak his language. We worked on bringing out his voice, his unique perspective on the research. We created a story that connected the audience to the science on an emotional level, and made them feel uplifted for being part of it. So Paul's success didn't just come from presenting his research; it came from telling his story in a way that resonated with the people listening.

In the end, Paul actually enjoyed giving his presentation. He felt surprisingly relaxed, even with a nasty cold! He made such an impression that people were still talking about it days later, with some even coming up to him just to say how great it was. A few said it was the best talk of the whole conference!

→ *For help building your presentation and story, see **Toolboxes 4 & 5***

Food for Thought

1. Where could a story help bring your talk to life?

→ *Think about and note down a place in your talk where a real example or personal insight could make your message clearer, more memorable, or more human.*

____

____

____

____

2. What was the most memorable talk you've ever listened to, and why?

→ *Was it the speaker's passion, their humour, their honesty?*

→ *Did they use a story that made something abstract feel real?*

____

____

____

____

3. How could you apply some of those elements in your own talk?

→ *Is there something in their delivery or storytelling style that inspired you?*

→ *Could you try something similar while still being true to your own style and voice?*

____

____

____

____

4. Observe and learn from others. Watch TED talks or presentations in your own field. Pay attention to:

→ *The kinds of stories they tell*

→ *How those stories link back to their message*

____

____

____

____

Notes from a talk or speaker I found inspiring:

____

____

____

____

5. What can you take away from these examples?

→ *What works for them might just work for you too. Start small, be sincere, and connect with your audience as yourself.*

→ *One small storytelling idea I'll try this week:*

Chapter 3: Body, Voice, and Presence

3.1 The Power of Performance

When we talk about performance in presenting, we're not just referring to standing up and speaking; it's about bringing everything together. It's your voice, your gestures, the energy you bring into the room, and the way you physically and verbally deliver your message. Think of it like an orchestra: your words, pauses, and pacing are the instruments, while the tone of your voice and the gestures you use add depth and expression. All these elements combine to create an engaging, memorable experience for your audience.

So everything we discuss in this book, from clear speech and word stress to the rhythm of delivery, comes together here. When it's done well, you're not just delivering information, you're creating a connection and inviting your audience into a story. Performance techniques are especially useful to you as a non-native speaker, because they're compensatory tools you can rely on. Hand gestures, facial expressions, and the position of your body can all help clarify your message.

In this chapter, we'll explore some of the key aspects of performance that help clarify and bring your presentation to life: how to use your voice, how to work with your body, and how to engage your audience – whether you're in a one-on-one meeting or speaking to a packed room.

3.2 Move Your Body (But Not Too Much!)

Body language isn't just about hand gestures or facial expressions; it's a core part of how we communicate, especially when presenting. For non-native speakers, this becomes even more important. As I mentioned in 3.1, how you stand, move, and physically express yourself can dramatically impact whether your message lands.

If you feel nervous about presenting, you're in good company. (The next chapter is all about managing nerves — and for good reason!) The good news is that your body can help you. Positive body language — standing tall, smiling, and using purposeful gestures — projects confidence. It also creates a more relaxed, engaging atmosphere. The result works both ways: you feel calmer, and so does your audience.

A few things to try:

- **Open posture**: Keep your shoulders back and chest open. This not only makes you look confident, but helps you breathe more easily.
- **Eye contact**: This helps you connect and build trust. Aim to look at different people across the room without staring anyone down (more on this in 3.3 and 4.7).
- **Smile**: A genuine smile breaks the ice and makes you feel more at ease. Lifting your eyebrows slightly also makes you appear more open and friendly.
- **Nodding**: Use subtle nods to show you're listening or to emphasise agreement. It's a small movement that signals you're engaged and confident.
- **Hand gestures**: Use your hands to underline what you're saying. Women, in particular, are sometimes taught to be more reserved in their movements, but gestures used intentionally can help you come across as more confident and credible.
- **Posture while sitting**: Keep your back straight, feet flat on the floor, and arms relaxed. This helps you appear more attentive and grounded.

What to avoid:

- **Closed posture**: Whether you're sitting or standing, avoid crossing your arms or hiding your hands in your pockets.

- **Leaning** against a wall or an object, such as a table. This can make you look disengaged or unsure of yourself. Instead, stand tall and relaxed, with you weight evenly balanced.

What to Do With Your Hands and Arms

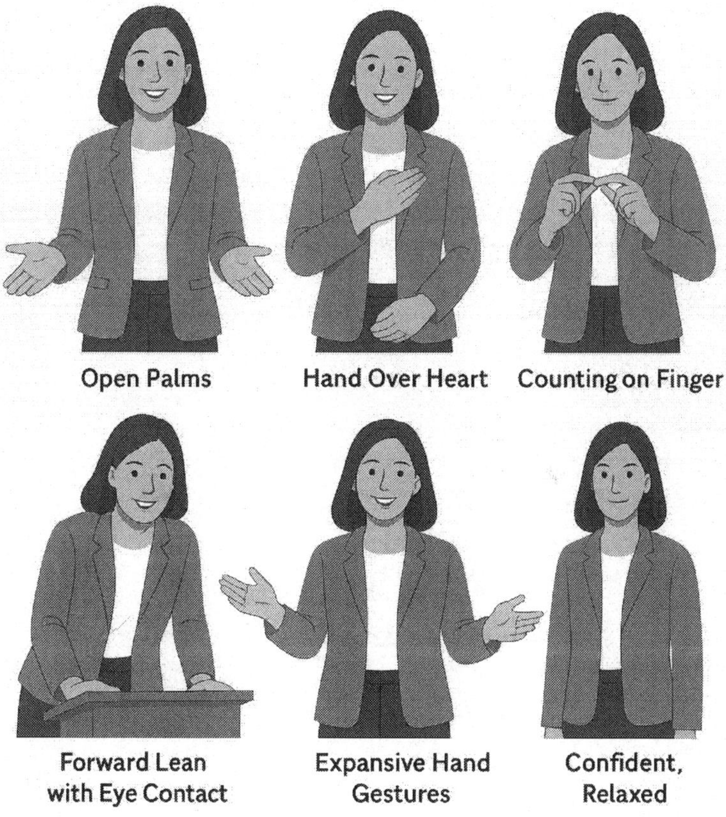

- **Open palms** signal honesty, openness, and lack of threat.
- **Hand over heart** shows sincerity and personal connection.
- **Counting on fingers** makes key points clear, structured, and easy to remember.

- **Forward lean with eye contact** shows engagement, draws the audience in, and adds emphasis.
- **Expansive hand gestures**. project confidence, energy, and authority while keeping attention focused on you.
- **Confident, relaxed posture** comes through when your arms rest loosely at your sides, or when you gently clasp your hands in front of your belly or diaphragm.

At first, these adjustments might feel a little awkward. That's normal. Over time, with regular practice, they'll start to feel more natural. The goal is to use body language in a way that supports your message – expressive, yet grounded.

If you're not used to using gestures or movement when you speak, start small. Try practising in front of a mirror or filming yourself to get a sense of how you come across. Focus on just one thing at a time – maybe adding a hand gesture when making a key point, or keeping your posture open and relaxed. As you get more comfortable, you can build from there. Think of it as developing a physical vocabulary that complements and supports your words.

3.3 Eye Contact and Engagement

Eye contact is one of the most powerful tools in public speaking and it can be especially helpful for non-native English speakers. It builds connection, confidence, and trust. When you meet someone's eyes during a presentation, you're saying: *I see you, and I'm here with you.*

That said, it's worth noting that **cultural norms vary**. In some cultures, direct eye contact is expected and shows confidence. In others, too much eye contact may be seen as confrontational. If you're presenting to an international or multicultural group, be mindful of this, and aim for gentle, respectful engagement. If eye contact feels intimidating, especially when you're speaking in a second language, you're by no means alone. Many people instinctively look down or glance away. But too little eye contact can give the impression of insecurity or disconnection.

A few ways to practise:

- **Rehearse in front of a mirror**, or record yourself to get comfortable. You could also practise in front of a trusted friend or family member.
- **Aim to make eye contact** with different sections of the audience throughout your talk, not just one person and certainly not the back wall.
- **For emphasis, make brief eye contact with someone when introducing a key idea** — it makes your message feel personal.
- **In online presentations, glance into the camera occasionally**, especially when making an important point. It helps your audience feel seen and keeps them engaged.

3.4 Using Gestures Effectively

Gestures help bring your words to life. They can clarify, highlight, and emphasise what you're saying — especially helpful when speaking in a second language.

But gestures aren't universal. A movement that feels expressive in one culture might come across as exaggerated or even confusing in another. For example, a thumbs-up is friendly in many places, but can be offensive elsewhere.

Two good general rules:

- **Know your audience**: A British or Japanese audience may prefer subtlety, while an American crowd might respond well to energetic gestures.
- **Avoid over-gesturing**: Too much movement can be distracting or feel unnatural.

The goal is for your gestures to *support* your message — not compete with it. For instance, when sharing a key statistic, you might raise your hand slightly or gesture outward to add emphasis. These small movements can help key points in your message stick with your audience.

3.5 Movement on Stage

It's not just your hands that speak, your whole body is part of your message. How and where you move can either add energy to your talk or distract from it.

One helpful way to think about movement is this: **move with meaning**. Walking across the stage for no reason can look like pacing. Pacing back and forth or moving restlessly on stage can distract and even unsettle the audience. But taking a step forward when you introduce a new idea, or shifting position to address a different part of the audience, adds structure and intention. Here are a few ideas to try:

- **Stand still during important points**. This grounds you and adds emphasis.
- **Move between sections of your talk**. This creates visual breaks and helps your audience follow your train of thought.
- **Use space to engage different areas of the room**. Good teachers, for example, often walk through the classroom when they are talking. This helps people feel included, especially in larger spaces.
- **Avoid swaying or shifting from foot to foot out of habit** (a lot of people do this without realising!). It's distracting and often a sign of nervous energy.

Again, balance is key. You don't have to choreograph every step, but being mindful of how you move can make your delivery more dynamic and confident.

3.6 Using Your Voice with Purpose

Your voice is just as expressive and powerful as your gestures. It's not about having a 'perfect' voice — it's about using the one you have with purpose and presence. Think of your voice as the emotional tone of your message. We've already explored storytelling in Chapter 2; it is here your voice becomes your strongest ally. A soft tone creates intimacy, a well-placed pause builds suspense, and a clear, confident voice signals: *I know what I'm talking about, and I want you to hear it.*

Voice-wise, focus on four main areas:

- **Pace**: Don't rush. Speaking too quickly makes it hard for people to follow, especially in a second language (see 1.9).
- **Pauses**: Give your audience time to absorb what you've said. Silence can be just as powerful as speech (again, see 1.9).
- **Intonation and Pitch**: Vary your pitch to keep things interesting. Avoid sounding monotonous, and let your natural expressiveness come through (see 1.7).
- **Projection**: Speak from your diaphragm — not your throat — to avoid strain and help your voice carry clearly.

Practise reading a passage out loud using different tones and pacing. It might feel silly, but it builds vocal awareness. Your voice doesn't just carry words — it carries emotion, intention, and credibility.

3.7 Interacting with Your Audience

Even if no one's speaking back, a presentation is a form of dialogue. How you interact with your audience shapes the experience, making it more dynamic and personal. You don't have to be overly extroverted. Just small moments of connection can make a big difference.

Try to:

- **Scan the room regularly**, making brief eye contact with different people.
- **Respond to their reactions**. If they smile, smile back. If they look puzzled, take a second to clarify.
- **Ask rhetorical questions or use inclusive phrases such as**:

  'So where does that leave us?'

  'But is this really enough?'

  'So where do we go from here?'

  'Let's take a look.'

  'We've all been there.'

  'We're all in the same boat.'
- **In smaller settings**, you might invite quick responses or comments. **In larger rooms**, it's more about tone and presence — making each listener feel like part of the conversation.

If you're online, things are a little different. You might not see everyone's face, but you can still create connection. Look into the camera occasionally, use people's names when responding, and make use of polls or chat functions if they're available.

3.8 Troubleshooting Common Body Language Challenges

Here are some common worries — one or two of which we're all likely to recognise!

- **Issue**: *I fidget when I'm nervous.*

  Solution: Give your hands a job: use them to gesture, hold a clicker, or rest them lightly in front of you. Try to keep them still during key moments to ground your energy.

- **Issue**: *I feel robotic when I try to use gestures.*

  Solution: Start with one or two simple movements tied to key points in your talk. With practice, they'll begin to feel more natural.

- **Issue**: *I don't know what to do with my feet.*

  Solution: Use your feet to really ground yourself. Stand with your feet shoulder-width apart for balance. Avoid shuffling or rocking.

- **Issue**: *I avoid eye contact.*

  Solution: Try glancing left, right, centre. This creates the impression of connection without being overwhelming.

- **Issue**: *I think I over-gesture.*

  Solution: Record and watch yourself on mute. Does it look too busy? Try slowing down your movements and using them more sparingly for key emphasis. Perhaps clasp your hands loosely in front of you, or hold a clicker or laser pointer.

In the Same Boat

You're not alone in any of this. Many professionals, even the most confident ones, find aspects of body language and presence challenging. Two of my clients, both very different personalities and speakers, worked through it in their own way:

Stephanie is a highly experienced business coach who really knows her stuff and expresses it with a dynamic, energetic style. But that same energy often showed up as restless gestures and excessive arm-waving, which tended to distract from her message.

We worked together on lowering her breathing and calming her system through gentle stretching exercises. These helped release excess adrenaline and brought a sense of stillness into her body. From there, we selected just a few key gestures she could use intentionally at specific points in her talk. If she felt she might start waving her arms again, she would clasp her hands together loosely in front of her diaphragm or belly.

We also developed a number of her core coaching insights into go-to stories — short, engaging narratives she could draw on in almost any situation. This proved especially helpful, as she's often invited to speak on YouTube podcasts and at various events. Calming her movements, combined with the clarity of those ready-made stories, helped her stay focused and present. With fewer, and more deliberate movements, her message now lands with much more impact — without the restless energy getting in the way.

Selin, a business analyst with an impressive CV, has a naturally strong and warm personality. But when speaking, she often came across as overly serious and a little distant. She had applied for several executive positions but never made it past the first interview. Selin rarely made eye contact and tended to hold back her smile, mostly due to tension. And yet, when she *did* smile, it lit up the whole room.

We worked on gentle de-stressing techniques and practised conscious smiling, and soft, intentional glances towards the interviewer. Through role play, we practised common interview scenarios and developed well-rounded answers to the questions she was most likely to face. Her confidence grew significantly, and when she was invited to a second interview, it gave her a real boost.

She didn't end up getting that particular job, but she was proud of how far she'd come, and more confident than ever that the right role would come her way. The final tip I gave her was to stay mindful of what she'd learned, and to keep practising to avoid slipping back into old habits.

Food for Thought

1. Feeling stiff?

→ *Try some gentle stretching, yoga, or shoulder rolls to release tension. Physical openness can lead to mental clarity and emotional ease.*

→ *Ask yourself:* Am I holding tension anywhere? Where might that tension be coming from?

____

____

____

____

2. Do you tend to back up or make yourself smaller?

→ *Try taking a deliberate step forward when you speak. You are allowed to be here. You're welcome in the space you take up.*

→ *Ask yourself:* When did I first start shrinking myself in certain situations? What would it feel like to take up more space with intention and ease?

____

____

____

____

3. What holds you back from being expressive?

→ *Is it fear of being 'too much'? Worry about being judged? A belief that people won't take you seriously? These are deeply human and worth exploring with compassion.*

→ *Ask yourself:* What do I associate with expressiveness? Do I link it with vulnerability, risk, or strength?

4. What does being 'too expressive' even mean?

→ *For some, it's big gestures. For others, it's showing emotion openly. There's no one-size-fits-all — just what feels true for you.*

→ *Ask yourself:* Where do I place myself on that spectrum? And who decided what was 'too much'?

5. What's the upside of expressing yourself more fully?

→ *Think of someone whose energy or emotion made a lasting impact on you. You can do that, too!*

→ *Ask yourself:* What would happen if I gave myself permission to do the same?

Chapter 4: Anxiety and How to Work With It

4.1 A Flight to Fear

In 2011, I found myself on a flight to Mallorca with my husband, our baby on my lap, and our preschooler happily seated between us. The plane hadn't left the ground, but my body was in total panic: sweaty palms, pounding heart, stomach in knots. It had been a whirlwind year — I was tired, overstretched, and, quite unexpectedly, gripped by a rising sense of dread. My mind was spinning in a familiar loop: *I'm trapped. I can't get out. I'm going to lose it. Everyone's going to see me fall apart and think I'm crazy.*

At the height of it, something both humiliating and miraculous happened. I unbuckled my seatbelt, passed our baby to my husband, and walked, almost breathless, down the aisle to the aircraft door, where a flight attendant stood. 'I'm getting off,' I blurted, my voice thin and shaky, barely under control.

For a moment, everything seemed to pause. The passengers nearby fell silent. Were they annoyed? Curious? Secretly wondering if this was a sign and they should get off too? Then the flight attendant looked at me — calm, kind — and said something I'll never forget: 'Of course you can get off. It's a beautiful day for flying; clear skies, smooth air. But if you want to leave, no problem. Entirely up to you.'

In that instant, something shifted. The intense fear that had been rising and rising suddenly eased. The moment he reminded me I had a choice, its grip loosened. To my own surprise, I stayed on the flight. Not that I felt great (far from it!), but it was certainly doable.

In hindsight, that moment taught me something profound: it's rarely the event itself that unravels us — it's feeling we're trapped. Whether it's flying or speaking in public, if we fear it, the stress response is the same. But the instant we reclaim even a little control, the body begins to settle, and fear starts to loosen its grip.

4.2 The Choice Game

That flight attendant understood something deeply powerful. Had he reacted with impatience or dismissal, I would have spiralled further. But because he remained calm and kind, and made me realise I had a choice, things changed significantly.

I realised I'd always used the 'choice game' with my students, and since then I've used it on myself and my clients too. When we feel anxious about speaking, we often feel trapped. We tell ourselves we *must* perform and there's no way out. The moment we believe we have no choice, panic can set in. But what if you gave yourself a way out — even if you don't take it?

Sometimes just knowing you have a choice can free you to move forward.

False beliefs often fuel what seems like unbearable panic. We convince ourselves that disaster is inevitable, that we will humiliate ourselves, or that others will judge us harshly. These thoughts feel real in the moment, but they are rarely true. Noticing when you are operating from a false belief is the first step toward loosening its grip.

The right self-talk is vital. Speak to yourself as you would to a friend: kindly, gently. And if you're really struggling, try this: imagine your adult self taking your child self by the hand. Picture yourself saying, *I know you're scared, and that's okay. You don't have to be perfect. I'm here with you*. That visualisation taps you into your adult self and is often enough to create a sense of calm and safety.

Whatever you do, do not get annoyed or angry with yourself for being nervous or afraid. **These feelings are totally human**. You're not doing anything wrong. You're doing your best, and you're allowed to take small steps, one at a time.

4.3 Everyone Feels It

You've probably heard the idea that some people are just 'naturally fearless' speakers, but this couldn't be further from the truth. It's easy to assume that confident public speakers are simply born that way, but many famous figures have struggled with nerves, even at the height of their careers.

Barack Obama, widely admired for his eloquence, has spoken openly about feeling nervous before big speeches and working hard to overcome his fear of public speaking in his early years. Similarly, Richard Branson has described himself as 'terrified' of speaking in public, despite being a globally recognised entrepreneur. Actress Nicole Kidman once said she used to be so shy, she could barely speak in public at all, yet she now regularly speaks on global stages.

What unites these individuals is **not an absence of fear, but a willingness to get on with it *despite* fear**. Each of them has found ways to relate to their nerves — whether through preparation, reframing, or practice — which allows them to speak *not without* nerves, but *despite* them. Their stories are a powerful reminder that anxiety doesn't have to be eliminated in order to speak with impact and authenticity.

For many of us, undoubtedly for famous people too, fear arrives in the form of '**what if' thoughts**:

- *What if I go blank?*
- *What if the audience hates me?*
- *What if I faint or completely mess up?*
- *What if I lose all credibility?*

One client told me, only half-jokingly, *'I hope I have an accident or get ill — then at least I won't have to do this presentation.'* Of course that's not their true voice talking. That's fear. And fear doesn't tend to speak in terms of truth; it speaks in *alarm bells*.

4.4 Preparing: Why and How

It might sound like a no-brainer — and for nervous speakers, even a bit of an anti-climax — when people say that thorough preparation helps combat nerves. It's a bit like telling someone who's afraid of flying to 'just get on the plane.' And yet, I'm always surprised by how many speakers try to skip this step. They often say they're too busy or have too much else on their plate. But the truth is, **thorough preparation is the one step you really cannot afford to skip**. All confident speakers practise — again and again and again. Not one of them gets up there and just wings it. Behind every seemingly effortless talk is a great deal of preparation, rehearsal, and refinement.

Thorough preparation gives you **a sense of control**. And if there's one thing that reduces anxiety, it's control. I always recommend writing your talk out **word for word**. Get it onto the page, say it out loud, and hear how it sounds. Then **practise, practise, practise**.

Some people worry this will make them sound robotic, but the opposite is actually true. **You're not memorising but internalising**. You're learning your content so well that it becomes part of who you are, part of your knowledge, your voice. Since this material is already part of your professional life, preparing it in this way actually **deepens your expertise**. As a result, it will seem as though you're speaking spontaneously, when in fact you're extremely well-prepared. As you'll see in Chapter 5, this is also hugely helpful in other speaking situations, like interviews and Q&A sessions.

But most importantly here, this kind of preparation is one of the most effective tools for managing fear. It doesn't eliminate nerves entirely, but it gives you something solid to stand on, and something to hang on to. At first, fear may take the upper hand, but with persistent practice, it gives way to enthusiasm and to the growing desire to share your talk with your audience, whether large or small.

Preparing well also means other things. If you know you're prone to anxiety, consider a few of these too:

- **Ease off caffeine** for a day or two beforehand. I personally love coffee, but it does *not* love my nervous system before a talk. You might be surprised how much it affects you. (As always, when it comes to your body or health, check what works for you.)
- **Get a good night's sleep**, but don't oversleep. Too much can leave you foggy and groggy.
- **Do something enjoyable beforehand**. Watch something funny, go for a walk, play a game. It reminds your brain: this talk is not my whole life.
- **Avoid stressful errands or chores** that drain your energy right before you speak.
- **Stretch, breathe, hydrate**. Gentle yoga stretches are the best, especially for your upper body (think neck, shoulders, and upper back). Low belly breathing and relaxed posture help more than most people realise. And make sure you stay hydrated! Dehydration can leave you sluggish and even trigger anxiety.
- **Create small personal rituals to help steady yourself**. These don't have to be elaborate, just simple actions that signal safety and calm to your body. For example, one of my clients presses her thumb and forefinger together whenever she feels tension rising; that tiny gesture helps her release the pressure and refocus. Another client chews gum beforehand, which works the same way for them — providing comfort and grounding right when they need it most.
- **Check out the venue**. If your presentation, talk or speech is in person, visit the room ahead of time if possible. Know where the exits are, where the audience will be, and how it feels to stand there and take command of the space. I personally find this incredibly effective – it's something I'm always sure to do.

- **Visualise connecting with the audience**. Imagine the room filled, every seat taken. Picture people chatting, laughing, and settling in. Imagine yourself smiling, laughing and even enjoying the whole thing. Then lower your breathing and say to yourself: '**I can handle anything that comes my way**.' I first came across this affirmation in Susan Jeffers' book *Feel the Fear and Do It Anyway* and I've found it to be incredibly powerful.

- **See if you can secure your preferred speaking slot**. Many people — myself included — really, *really* dislike the waiting, so we prefer to go first. Other popular spots are second and last. More on that in 4.8.

- **Practise low belly breathing, especially in the minutes before you speak**. It calms your nervous system, grounds your voice, and slows your heart rate. Combine this with slowing your speech just slightly, and using purposeful pauses to gather your thoughts (see: 1.9). These pauses not only help you feel composed, but give your audience time to take in what you're saying.

- **Skip ahead in time**. Here's a trick that many people find surprisingly helpful: imagine the moment after your talk is done. For example, picture yourself sitting down with a nice cup of coffee and your cat on your lap, feeling that sweet sense of relief. You did it. It's behind you. You got through it and the world didn't end. In fact, you might even feel a little proud of yourself. Let that image carry you forward. Sometimes skipping ahead in time helps remind you that the talk is just one moment, and life keeps moving afterwards.

4.5 Change Your Thoughts, Change Your Mind

It is essential to realise that your thoughts directly affect your nervous system. The way you think can either calm your body or send it into high alert. When your brain senses threat, whether physical or imagined, it prepares your body to act: fast heartbeat, shallow breath, shaky hands, dry mouth, and that overwhelming urge to escape. These reactions are part of your fight-or-flight response. It's your system trying to protect you, even when the 'danger' is just speaking up in a meeting in English. For non-native speakers, the thoughts that trigger this reaction are often specific:

- *What if I forget the right word in English?*
- *What if I make a grammar mistake, or use a wrong word and sound stupid?*
- *What if my pronunciation is off and they don't understand me?*
- *What if they judge me for my accent or think I'm not professional enough?*
- *What if I make a complete fool of myself and faint?*
- *What if I lose my train of thought, go blank, and forget how to speak English at all?!*

These thoughts are completely normal, but left unchecked, they grow louder and more powerful. And the longer you try to silence them or push them away, the more energy they gain. So what can you do?

Here's a surprisingly effective approach. Don't fight the fear: first accept it, and if it persists, then *invite it in* (yes, really). This approach is explained at length in the book *Dare* by Barry McDonagh. Let's take a closer look at how to do this:

Step 1: Normalise it

Start by saying: *'Ah, there you are again. Hello, fear.'* Don't get caught up in it. Don't give it extra meaning. It's just a familiar old visitor. *'You always show up before I speak. That's fine. I know you.'* Remember, fear only becomes overwhelming when you believe it's a problem. When you treat it like an emergency, your body reacts accordingly. But when you greet it calmly, it loses power and your body calms down — oftentimes immediately.

Step 2: Invite more

This might sound counterintuitive, but if the fear persists, lean into it — ask for more. Say to yourself, *'Is that all you've got? Come on then, give me more. Show me your worst.'* By doing this, you're signalling that you're not intimidated by the fearful feelings; in fact, you're showing that their presence doesn't matter to you.

What often happens is remarkable: the fear begins to recede. In my experience — and in the experiences of many people I've taught — this approach causes the feelings to rise, but when you invite them in and ask for more, they quickly lose intensity and sink away.

Step 3: Get on with it

After that? Shrug and move on. Pay it no attention. Let the nerves sit quietly in the background while you focus on what really matters: your message, your story, your audience. This may surprise you, but you don't need to feel fearless to do something meaningful. You just need to stop letting fear take the lead.

Now let's reframe some of those classic 'what if' thoughts. Try this:

- *What if I freeze?* → Then I'll pause, take a breath, glance at my notes, and carry on.
- *What if they judge me?* → Some people might, but most will be supportive and want you to succeed. When this fear comes up, remind yourself that everyone judges from time to time. It's a normal human response and doesn't define your worth or abilities – or anyone else's for that matter.
- *What if I mess up in English?* → So what? I'll laugh, take a breath, and keep going.
- *What if they don't understand me?* → Then I'll rephrase. That's part of communication.
- *What if I look nervous?* → Who cares? Nerves are normal. And if people notice, they'll likely empathise.

- *What if I faint on stage?* → Someone will come and help me, that's what people do. The event will go on, and so will life.

Fear thrives on unfinished stories, so you really need to finish them (consider this truth deeply for a moment!). Finish them out loud, in writing, or with a trusted friend or family member. And then just get on with whatever it is you need to do. The fear might be screaming in the background, but it won't stay for long once it realises you're not listening anymore.

It's Not Fear, It's Excitement!

Years ago, I saw an empowerment trainer on *The Oprah Winfrey Show* working with people who were terrified of heights. He had them stand atop a tall wooden zip-line platform and shout, 'I'm excited!' multiple times before gliding down. Strange as it sounds, it actually makes sense.

Fear and excitement are really just two sides of the same coin; they're both forms of nervous arousal. The body's stress response to something we label as 'scary' is almost identical to its response to something we label as 'exciting.' That's why roller coasters and scary films can feel both terrifying and exhilarating at the same time. By reframing fear as excitement, you can shift how your brain interprets what's happening in your body.

You won't see me sliding down zip lines or riding on roller coasters any time soon, but I do use this approach myself. I'm still fearful of flying, so every time I board a plane, I deliberately tell myself how excited I am and how amazing it is that I get to do this. It doesn't make me entirely comfortable, but it does get me on that plane — and even laughing at my own fear.

So next time you're about to speak English in front of an audience, tell yourself, *'I'm excited to do this. I can't wait to get up there and share.'* The brain is surprisingly easy to fool – so see what happens when it starts to believe the new things you're telling it.

4.6 Redirect Your Focus

When we're nervous, our focus often turns sharply inward. We get so caught up in our own fear — our physical sensations, our imagined shortcomings and mistakes — that we forget why we're speaking in the first place. Our inner dialogue can be relentless: *What will they think of me? Will I mess up? Do I sound strange? Am I good enough?* This probably all sounds very familiar!

Sadly, when our energy is directed towards **how we're being perceived**, anxiety naturally grows. It's like shining a spotlight on yourself and then trying to relax under the heat. Luckily, **you can move that spotlight.** Sometimes, the most powerful shift is also the simplest. Remind yourself of the following, over and over again:

→ *It's not about me.*
→ *It's about my message.*

That's exactly what one client said to me after a major presentation. She'd been paralysed by nerves just before it was her turn to speak. But the moment she remembered her purpose — the reason she was sharing her ideas in the first place — something clicked. 'It's not about me,' she told herself, 'It's about the message.' And that shift helped her accept the nerves with relative ease. So the next time you feel caught in your own head, try challenging your thoughts. Instead of asking yourself how you will be judged, ask yourself:

→ *What do I want to share?*
→ *Who might need to hear this today?*
→ *How can I serve or connect with this audience?*

Fear thrives on ego: not in a boastful sense, but in the *self-focused* sense. When we **turn our attention outward** — to the people in front of us, to the story we're telling, to the idea we're standing for — we take the pressure off ourselves and place our attention where it belongs, namely on connection. It doesn't mean you won't feel nervous. But it does mean your nervousness won't be the boss. As Janet E. Esposito so beautifully puts it in her book *In the Spotlight*, '**your**

purpose is not to gain the approval of others, but to add value to the lives of others.' Remind yourself of this constantly. Write it on Post-it notes and stick them on your bathroom mirror if you have to.

Also, **be mindful of how you talk to yourself after the event**. This is vital. If you've been nervous, don't focus on this, don't beat yourself up about it. Focus on the fact that you got up in front of that audience and did it. Tell yourself you did the best you could do and that you're taking steps to get even better.

4.7 Be the Caring Host

Once, in my first job as a teacher, I was preparing to give a talk to a group of parents. I was nervous — nauseous, sweaty palms, the whole lot. As people filtered into the room, a woman approached me quietly and said, *'I don't like crowds. I'd really like to sit near the door.'*

That stopped me in my tracks. *She* was nervous in this situation too. Something in me immediately shifted: I stopped focusing on myself and started thinking *How can I help her feel safe and welcome?* So I said, 'Of course, I understand. And if you need to leave at any point, please feel completely free to do so.' She smiled gratefully and, as it turned out, stayed for the entire talk.

This was an absolute turning point for me, and one I think of often. You see, I realised I wasn't just a speaker. I was the host, just as that airline flight attendant had been *my* host. It was my job to create ease, not just for myself, but for the people in the room. It also reminded me that we're all basically in the same boat, but with different roles. Believe it or not, some people actually feel more comfortable on stage than in the audience!

The following small actions can have a big impact, not just on how you feel, but on the connection you build with your audience. Think of them as your anchors. They're easy to try, and often surprisingly effective:

- **Connect with others**. An organiser, a fellow speaker, a facilitator, such as someone arranging the catering. These small connections remind you: *I'm not alone in this.*

- **If you can, stand at the door before your talk and greet people as they arrive**. Smile, nod, say hello, maybe even have a short chat or two. It's an excellent way to ground yourself, break the tension, and shift from nervous speaker to friendly host.

- **While you're speaking, look for friendly faces in the room**, those who seem relaxed, encouraging, or interested. Gently return to them now and then. This way they become your little anchors, your quiet cheerleaders. Just don't lock eyes or stare people down; soft, brief glances are more than enough to create connection.

- **Ignore the popular advice to 'look over the audience**.' I never recommend this. It might feel safer (personally, I don't think so), but it also tunes you out of the room. You lose the warmth, the presence, and the very human interaction that makes your message land and eases your nerves. More importantly, it makes you feel very alone.

- **Don't tell the audience you're nervous**. This advice is often given, but I'm not a fan. While it might seem honest or disarming, it usually backfires: it can make both you and your audience feel awkward, draw attention to your nerves rather than your message, and actually heighten your anxiety. Instead, focus on grounding yourself: take a breath, pause, and begin confidently (fake it before you feel it, if need be). Most audiences won't notice your nerves unless you tell them.

4.8 Waiting is Harder Than Doing

Many people struggle with what's called **anticipatory anxiety**: the intense nervousness that arises before a speaking engagement, sometimes weeks or even months in advance. For some, these feelings can be overwhelming, even paralysing.

Interestingly, the anxiety often eases once the moment has arrived and you begin speaking. Beforehand, your mind tends to run wild, imagining everything that might go wrong. But when you're actually in the moment, reality sets in and you come to realise there's nothing frightening about the audience. They're not a pack of hungry wolves, and most of them actually want you to succeed.

If this sounds familiar, make it a habit to remind yourself of this truth. Tell yourself: *I can do this. The waiting is harder than the doing. Once I start, I'll settle and manage just fine.*

As I mentioned in 4.4, it's often worth aiming for your preferred speaking slot. Going first lets you get it over with quickly so you can relax and enjoy the rest of the event. Going second means someone else has already broken the ice for you. And if you're last, you can take comfort in knowing the end is in sight.

Remember: public speaking is not something to survive, it's a fun and exciting thing to be part of. These small shifts in your thinking can make a world of difference. Suffering from stage fright doesn't mean there's anything wrong with you; it's totally human and something millions of people struggle with. But the more you work with it — gently, consistently, non-judgementally — the more it shifts. Ask for feedback. Notice what went well and keep showing up. Each time you speak, you grow; not just as a communicator, but as a person. And the more you speak up, the more others will find the courage to do the same.

In the Same Boat

Honestly, everyone I've ever worked with has needed help with speaking nerves at some point. You're definitely not alone in this, not by a long shot.

You've probably noticed in this chapter that I've shared lots of different ways to deal with nerves, and that's very intentional. There isn't a one-size-fits-all solution. What works beautifully for one person might not click at all for someone else. That's why I always work with my clients to figure out what feels right for *them* — something that suits their personality and feels natural, rather than forced.

Let's take Louise, a French-Canadian HR specialist working in an international company, who came to me because she felt extremely anxious about speaking up in meetings. She described how nervous she felt just before opening her mouth, so much so that her voice often came out pinched and halted, and her words didn't land the way she wanted them to. 'I sound like I'm about to cry or run away,' she told me. 'And the more I hear myself sound that way, the worse it gets.'

Together, we worked on a few simple but powerful strategies, beginning with the body. Before meetings, I asked Louise to take a moment to breathe deeply into her belly, rather than letting the breath stay high in her chest. This kind of low, grounded breathing helps calm the nervous system and stabilises the voice. We paired it with a technique I often recommend: yawning gently just before speaking (you can do this without people noticing). Try it now and notice how it opens the space at the back of your throat. That's exactly the feeling to aim for when you speak.

We also worked on relaxing the jaw and softening the shoulders, and imagining her voice travelling from deep in her chest, rather than being squeezed out of a tight throat. These are small adjustments, but together, they help the voice sound fuller, warmer, and more confident. The change in Louise wasn't instant, but it was certainly steady. Over time, her voice became more fluid and grounded. She didn't just sound more confident, she actually *felt* it. 'Now I actually want to speak up,' she said one day, almost surprised. 'It still takes effort, but it doesn't feel like a dangerous emergency anymore.' And that's the goal. Not to erase the nerves completely, but to work *with* them, and speak with clarity, calm, and just a little more ease.

→ *For help troubleshooting common speaking situations, see* ***Toolbox 9***

Food for Thought

1. What does fear feel like for you?

→ *How does it show up in your body? (e.g. sweaty palms, racing heart, shallow breath, wobbly knees, shaky hands)*

→ *What thoughts tend to come with it? Are there any familiar 'what if' statements you've noticed?*

____

____

____

____

2. What do you say to yourself when you're nervous?

→ *Is your inner voice kind, harsh, panicked, practical...?*

____

____

____

____

→ *What would it sound like if you spoke to yourself like a trusted friend? I'd like it to sound more like:*

3. Try completing a 'what if' thought you often have:

→ *E.g. 'What if I forget my words?'*

→ *'Then I'll pause, check my notes, and carry on.'*

4. Skip ahead in time

→ *What will you do after your talk or presentation? What will that moment feel like? A walk? A warm drink? A text from a friend? Paint that picture in your mind — it helps bring perspective.*

5. Your message and your why

→ *What do you want your audience to walk away with?*

→ What matters more than your fear? This matters because:

6. One thing I'll try next time to make myself feel at ease:

→ Could be a breathing exercise, a walk beforehand, a smile at the door, or a quick reminder: 'It's not about being perfect — it's about showing up.'

Chapter 5: Finding Your English Voice in Every Setting

5.1 Preparation is More Than Just Practice

When it comes to job interviews, promotion interviews, small talk, or Q&A sessions, many people assume it's all about having the perfect words and flawless grammar. For non-native speakers, this understandably becomes the main focus area. And yes, as we will see later on in this chapter, preparing what you say matters. But it's not just about *what* you say. It's equally about *how* you show up: your posture, your energy, your eye contact, your facial expressions, and how you connect with the person or people in front of you.

The tools in this chapter can support you — even compensate a little — if you're still working on your English language skills. A calm, confident presence, clear body language, and a friendly tone can go a long way in helping you make a strong, professional impression.

Whether the meeting is online or in person, your presence speaks before you even say a word. And it can work in your favour, even if the language feels tricky.

5.2 Online vs. In-Person

It's easy to underestimate online meetings and interviews. You're at home, sitting in a familiar chair, perhaps using the same laptop you use for emails or Netflix. That comfort can make people a little too relaxed: slouching, looking off-screen, or showing up in a jumper that says *Sunday mood* instead of *Monday mind-set*.

Here's a quick checklist for online interactions:

- **Sit up straight**. It helps you breathe more easily and makes you look alert.

- **Keep an open body position**. Avoid folding your arms across your chest, which can signal defensiveness. In an interview — or any presentation or conversation — you want to appear approachable. Instead, clasp your hands loosely in front of you and keep your shoulders straight.
- **Use natural hand gestures**. Gestures help emphasise points. When you're not using your hands, rest them lightly together in front of you.
- **Look towards the camera when speaking**. This simulates eye contact and keeps your listener engaged.
- **Dress appropriately**. Head to toe, in case you need to stand up.
- **Silence your mobile**. Notifications or message alerts are distracting and can make you appear unfocused.
- **Check your background and lighting**. Keep it free of clutter and distractions.

In face-to-face meetings, your presence is judged the moment you walk through the door — eye contact, handshake (if culturally appropriate), posture, tone of voice, and overall energy all matter. The same applies online. **The simplest is to treat an online interview just like an in-person one**. However the meeting takes place, the way you present yourself sets the tone.

5.3 Preparing for Job Interviews

You can usually predict the kinds of questions you'll be asked; you just need to think ahead. Most interviews and Q&A sessions cover a few familiar themes, and preparing for these will help you stay calm, focused, and let your English flow naturally.

Here are some of the questions you're most likely to hear in a job or promotion interview:

→ *Tell me about yourself.*

→ *Why do you want to work here (specifically this company or organisation)?*

→ *What attracted you to this role?*

→ *What are your strengths and weaknesses?*

→ *Describe a challenge you've faced and how you handled it.*

→ *How do you handle tight deadlines?*

→ *How do you handle conflict in the workplace?*

→ *What makes you a good fit for this position or team?*

→ *Where do you see yourself in two to five years?*

A lot of people struggle with this part of the interview. They've got all the right experience, but when it comes to answering these standard questions, they either **say far too much** or **hardly anything at all**. What they often do:

- Ramble and go off on tangents, sharing every detail of their career history or life story.
- Or give such a short reply that the interviewer learns nothing about them.

This may be something you struggle with too. Here's how you can fix it:

Focus on only answering the question being asked, not everything you *could* say.

- Build clear, concise answers that highlight your most relevant experience or strengths.
- Practise out loud so the answers sound natural, not rehearsed.
- Practise slowing down to avoid rushing and rambling.

Now let me show you the difference.

Example question #1: 'Tell me about yourself.'

Answer that goes all over the place:

'I grew up in Buenos Aires and then moved around a lot because my dad worked for an international company, and I guess that's why I'm so adaptable. I started working in the hospitality branch, then I travelled and worked in Europe, which was amazing because I got to see lots of different cultures. I've always been interested in people and how things work, so that's why I studied psychology, and I thought I might be a teacher, but I didn't go through with it. Eventually I found myself in HR, which I love, although I've also thought about going back into the hospitality branch as a manager at some point. Anyway, in my free time I do yoga and weight lifting, and I love travelling.'

Answer that says hardly anything:

'I'm hardworking and get along well with people. I think I'd do a good job here.'

A good answer (focused and natural):

'I've spent the last five years working in HR, mainly in recruitment and employee engagement. I first worked in the hospitality sector, where I looked after everything from onboarding new staff to running training sessions. More recently, I've taken on extra responsibility for improving HR processes.

What I enjoy most is helping make people's working lives smoother and more rewarding; that's one of the reasons I'm so interested in this role. I really like your company's focus on professional development, because I think supporting people to grow is one of the best ways to keep them motivated and performing well.'

Example question #2: 'How do you handle tight deadlines?'

Answer that goes all over the place:

'I've always been good with deadlines. I suppose it started at university, where I had to juggle essays, part-time jobs, and sports. I also volunteered at an animal shelter. I remember one time I stayed up three nights in a row to finish a project, and even though I was exhausted, I managed to get it done. In my last job, there were always urgent tasks; once we even had to deliver something in just 24 hours, which was stressful but we pulled through. I usually just do my best to prioritise, and I think I'm naturally calm under pressure, so I guess that helps too.'

Answer that says hardly anything:

'I just work faster. I don't mind deadlines.'

A good answer (focused and natural):

'When I have a tight deadline, I start by looking at what needs to be done first and what can wait. I share the plan with my colleagues straight away, so everyone knows what's happening and there are no surprises. I also keep checking progress as we go, so I can change things quickly if something unexpected happens.

For example, in my last job we had a last-minute client request that cut our usual timeline in half. I reorganised the tasks and shared them across the team, and we still delivered on time without losing quality. I've noticed I work well under pressure: deadlines help me focus and find solutions quickly.'

Practise answering out loud and ideally record yourself. Listening back isn't about criticising yourself; it's about noticing where your story could be clearer, more concise, or better structured. That awareness alone makes a huge difference to your confidence.

Golden tip for young professionals starting out: Recently, an HR client mentioned something interesting that I'd like to share with you here. Many young applicants, she said, tend to focus on their weak points — on what they don't know. Do not do this. Instead, focus on what you *do* know, on the skills and strengths you already bring to the table, and on the fact that you are willing and eager to learn what you don't know yet.

This shift in perspective can make a huge difference. Employers aren't looking for someone who's perfect; they're looking for someone who's capable, positive, and open to growth. When you present yourself this way, you come across as confident and teachable, which is far more appealing than listing all the things you still need to improve.

Do Your Homework

Regularly, clients come to the session to practise for an upcoming interview feeling prepared, but when I ask them to tell me about the company or organisation they're applying to... *silence*. Often, they have only looked at the job description and requirements. But getting to know the company is just as important. So make sure you take time to:

- **Read the company's website**: especially their mission, values, and recent news.
- **Look up your interviewers on LinkedIn**: what is their position at the company or in the organisation?
- **Check if the organisation has published anything recently**: a report, articles, posts on LinkedIn etc.

I always recommend having a few thoughtful questions ready — not just to impress, but to take the lead for a moment. It shows you're curious, enthusiastic, and genuinely interested. Try:

→ *What do you enjoy most about working here?*
→ *How would you describe the team culture?*
→ *What would success in this role look like after six months?*

Doing this extra research not only helps you stand out but also makes you feel more confident going into the interview. When you understand the people and the organisation you're speaking to, your answers feel more grounded, your questions more meaningful, and the whole conversation becomes a two-way exchange rather than an interrogation.

For **promotion interviews**, many of the questions will feel similar to those in a standard job interview, but with one important twist: the focus will often be on your performance in your current role. You might be asked to talk through a specific case, project, or challenge you've handled – either something you managed particularly well or a situation that didn't go as planned and what you learned from it.

This is your chance to show not only your skills, but also your growth and readiness to take on greater responsibility. Be prepared to highlight how you've contributed to your team's success, built relationships, solved problems, and developed new skills since stepping into your current position. Concrete examples from your day-to-day work can make a big impact here, especially if they show how you've already been operating at the level of the role you're seeking. Make sure you prepare and practise these examples well.

5.4 Small Talk and the FORD method

Some clients tell me they're comfortable speaking in English about their job or area of expertise, but when someone asks what they did at the weekend, things suddenly get awkward. A lot of people don't particularly enjoy small talk (I'm one of them), but small talk is an important social skill to break the ice and connect with others.

In interviews, and at work generally, small talk is a powerful way to build rapport. It creates a human moment and opens the door to trust. It makes people feel seen, heard, and included. Practising small talk on everyday, non-work topics can really help you feel more confident and natural when conversations begin.

Here are some safe, easy topics to start with:

- The weather (always a classic!)
- A film you recently watched
- A book you're reading
- A weekend walk or trip you've taken
- Local traditions or festivals
- A holiday you're planning or have just returned from
- An interesting article you read on LinkedIn

If you feel uncomfortable talking about yourself first, you can start by asking the other person a simple question. Often, they'll answer, and then ask you the same question in return, which makes it easier to join in.

Let me take this opportunity to highlight something many people overlook: the power of listening. I cannot stress enough how important real, deep listening is.

When you truly listen — rather than just waiting for your turn to speak — the entire exchange changes. It helps you pick up on details you can respond to, makes the other person feel valued, and naturally keeps the conversation flowing. Listening well often does more to build connection than anything clever you could say.

The FORD Method

A simple way to remember small talk topics is the FORD method, developed by customer service consultant and author John DiJulius. Here it is:

F – Family

- *'Where's your family based?'* or *'Where do most of your family members live?'*
- *'What kinds of things do you enjoy doing with your family?'*

O – Occupation

- *'What do you enjoy most about your work?'*
- *'How did you first get into your field?'*

R – Recreation (hobbies, free time)

- *'What do you usually do to relax at the weekend?'*
- *'Have you picked up any new hobbies recently?'*

D – Dreams (future plans or goals)

- *'What's something special you're working on right now?'*
- *'What's something you'd love to try in the future?'*

Notice how most of these questions invite a longer answer rather than just 'yes' or 'no'. Closed questions, such as '*Do you have a family*?' or '*Do you like your job*?' can short-circuit the conversation. **Open-ended questions** give the other person space to share more, which makes it easier for you to respond and keep things flowing.

Making Small Talk More Interesting

To sound more fluent and engaging, try adding **phrases and expressions** that give simple topics a bit more colour:

Weather

- *'The weather can't seem to make up its mind today!'*
- *'I hope the weather behaves itself this weekend.'*
- *'It's four seasons in one day at the moment.'*
- *'At least it's brightening up; it was miserable earlier.'*

Films

- *'I finally got round to watching (film/series/documentary title) — it was better than I expected.'*

- *'Have you seen anything good lately? I need recommendations.'*
- *'It's the kind of film you think about long after it ends.'*

Books

- *'I'm halfway through (book title) — I honestly can't put it down.'*
- *'Do you like thrillers? This one has such a clever twist.'*
- *'It's one of those books you want to tell everyone about.'*

Weekends / Trips

- *'I went for a walk at (place name); it was exactly what I needed.'*
- *'We found a great little café; I'll have to take you there sometime.'*
- *'It felt good to switch off for a bit and get outdoors.'*

Festivals / Local Traditions

- *'There's such a nice buzz around town during (festival name).'*
- *'It's one of those events everyone looks forward to each year.'*
- *'The atmosphere was great. The music, the food, everything.'*

Holidays

- *'We've just booked a trip to (place name) — I can't wait.'*
- *'We've just come back from (place name); it was amazing to unplug for a week.'*
- *'It's somewhere I've always wanted to visit, so I'm excited.'*

Tip to keep the chat flowing:

Once they answer, show you're listening by adding a little follow-up. For example:

→ *'That sounds lovely. How often do you get to do that?'*

→ *'Wow, I've heard (place name) is amazing. What did you like most about it?'*

→ *'I've been meaning to try that myself. Would you recommend it?'*

A short comment or question like this shows genuine interest and helps the conversation keep going naturally. **For expats, small talk is also a valuable way to integrate into a new culture**. Learning about local customs, holidays, or foods not only helps you connect more easily, but shows respect for the place you're living in. It's also a great way to broaden your horizons at the same time.

→ *For some vocab for everyday conversations, see **Toolbox 6***
→ *If you're mingling with native speakers, you may also find **Toolbox 7** useful*

In the Same Boat

Christina is a highly intelligent medical professional from Greece. In her own language, she's an excellent conversationalist. But when she came to me, she was working in New York and found herself struggling socially. She could comfortably talk about her profession, but when it came to more personal topics, she felt awkward and hesitant.

Outside of work, she mostly socialised with other Greek people, yet she longed to connect with American locals too. She wanted to move beyond small talk about the weather and share more meaningful moments to be able to tell a funny story, join in group conversations, and participate even when the topic touched on cultural references she didn't yet know.

We started by working on a simple story structure: a beginning, middle, and ending with a light punchline. This helped her frame personal anecdotes in a way that felt natural and engaging.

Together, we watched American and British comedians and celebrities on YouTube to study how they tell stories: their timing, facial expressions, and the way they use pauses to make their stories land.

From there, Christina began to practise in small, manageable ways. She tried out short stories at the coffee machine with colleagues at the hospital, sharing little moments from her weekend. She also started listening more closely to others; not just to understand the words, but to notice their tone, reactions, and what mattered to them. This helped her see where she could join in, add encouragement, or connect her own experiences to theirs.

What had once felt like a huge hurdle started to feel fun. She found that connecting with people in English, not just in professional settings but socially as well, began to feel easier and far more natural. She joined in more, and even started being invited to dinner and get-togethers. Slowly her world in New York opened up in a way that felt richer and more enjoyable than she'd imagined possible.

5.5 Pitching

Pitching can feel intimidating. Many people hear the word and picture standing in front of a crowd, trying to 'sell' themselves. In reality, a pitch is simply a clear, engaging way of telling someone who you are, what you do, why it matters, and — importantly — what you're looking for. Here is an overview of different types of pitches:

Business & Startups

- Presenting your startup idea to investors
- Convincing partners to back your product launch

Workplace & Projects

- Proposing a new workflow or tool to your manager
- Suggesting a creative campaign in a marketing meeting

Sales & Client Work

- Selling a product or service to a potential customer
- Offering a tailored solution in response to a client's needs

Creative Industries

- Presenting a book idea to a publisher
- Pitching a movie concept to a studio
- Suggesting a storyline to a game development team

Competitions & Public Events

- Entering a pitch competition to win funding or support
- Advocating for your idea at a hackathon

Internal Team Buy-in

- Trying to get coworkers excited about your approach
- Requesting resources for your project from higher-ups

In all these cases, the goal is the same: present an idea clearly, persuasively, and in a way that makes the listener want to say 'yes.'

Including Your Why

The 'why' in a pitch is powerful. As Simon Sinek points out, people don't just buy what you do – they connect with why you do it. Your motivation or belief can be just as compelling as your skills or experience. Keep it short and human. Share what you do, who you help, why you care about it, and what you hope will happen next – whether that's getting advice, an introduction, or simply staying in touch. For example, I might say:

'I'm a teacher and public speaking coach, and I help people become confident speakers in English. I've always loved helping people find their voice in English and blossom; seeing them go from hesitant to

expressive is incredibly rewarding. Right now, I'm looking to connect with companies that want to support their teams' English communication skills.'

Notice how simple that is? It's not about impressing people; it's about making them curious and starting a real conversation. When you pitch from your 'why' and clearly state what you want, it doesn't feel like selling — it feels like sharing something meaningful.

A Simple Framework for Your Pitch

Try this four-part structure:

1. **I am**... (your role or identity)
2. **I help**... (who you help and how)
3. **I care because**... (your why; why it matters to you)
4. **I'm looking for**... (what you want: advice, feedback, connection, opportunity)

Mini-tip: **Learn from 'Shark Tank**.' If you want to see business pitches — both good and not-so-good — in action, watch a few episodes of *Shark Tank* (or *Dragons' Den* in the UK). As you watch, apply this simple framework and see who does it well:

- Do they clearly explain who they are?
- Do they make it obvious who they help and why?
- Do they share a sense of passion or purpose behind what they do?
- Do they clearly state what they want from the people they're pitching to?

You'll notice that the most interesting pitches aren't always the ones with the flashiest products. Often, they're the ones where the 'why' is clear, the ask is direct, and the connection feels real. You'll also see pitches that could improve instantly by adding this human element.

That said, it's important to know that not all audiences are interested in your 'why.' Some care more about what's in it for them.

So, include it when:

- **You're building trust or emotional connection**: people remember why you care more than just what you offer.
- **The audience values authenticity**: early-stage investors, nonprofit boards, or creative collaborators often want to know your personal motivation.
- **Your why strengthens your credibility**: if your motivation shows commitment or relevant experience ('I started this app because I struggled with the same problem for years'), it makes you more believable.

And leave it out when:

- **Your why overshadows the solution**: if you spend too long on your story, you may run out of time to show the value of your idea.
- **The audience is purely metrics-driven**: some corporate buyers or procurement managers want ROI (return on investment), timelines, and proof — not a heartfelt origin story.
- **Your why feels irrelevant**: if your personal motivation doesn't connect to the problem you're solving, it can distract rather than inspire.

→ *For help writing your pitch, see **Toolbox 8***

5.6 Handling Q&A Sessions

For many of my clients, the Q&A part of a presentation or meeting causes the most stress, often even more than the presentation itself.

It's the moment you're no longer in control of the questions. But remember that Q&A is just a conversation, not a test. Try to think of it as a chance to connect and clarify, not a trap to fall into. Your audience is curious, and that's a good thing. It means they're engaged. Anticipate what might come up:

- What parts of your talk might prompt further questions?
- What might need extra clarification?
- Have colleagues or clients asked similar things before?

Ask a trusted friend or colleague to quiz you in advance and prepare answers that you can lean on, much like preparing for a job interview (see 5.3).

How to respond confidently:

- **Pause before answering**. This shows you're thoughtful and gives you time to gather your words.

- **Mind your breathing**. Make sure it's low in the belly, not high in the chest. Also consciously relax your shoulders.

- **Use simple, clear language** (remember 2.6) — especially if you're feeling nervous. **Ask for clarification if needed**: 'Could you say that a different way?' or 'Do you mean...?

- **Use examples if it helps**. A quick story or real-life moment can make a big idea much clearer. Be sure to write and practise this beforehand.

- **Be honest if you don't know**. You can say: 'That's a good question — I'll need to look into that and get back to you.' That's not a sign of weakness; it's called being professional. I've done this many times myself, and it always earns respect rather than doubt.

In the Same Boat

Barry, a Dutchman, had a promotion interview coming up at an international energy company. He'd applied for the role before but had been rejected. The feedback he received was that he didn't seem 'mature' enough for the position. While Barry was clearly capable, he came across as a little too casual, in both how he carried himself and how he conducted the interview.

This time, he had one more chance — and understandably, he was nervous. Barry was hesitant at first. Like many people, he felt a little resistant to changing how he spoke and carried himself. That's perfectly human; sometimes change feels uncomfortable, even when we know it's necessary. But growth nearly always requires a bit of discomfort. And in Barry's case, being willing to lean into that change was exactly what allowed him to move forward.

The interview would again be online, and with the same panel as before. We began by recreating the first interview using role play. I noticed a few things immediately: he sat slightly slouched, looked down and to the side too often, and never once made eye contact with the camera. There was also a lot of searching for words, which revealed a lack of preparation.

We started working on the essentials. I encouraged him to sit up straight, prepare his answers more carefully, and speak more slowly and thoughtfully. Many of the techniques we practised are covered in Chapter 1, such as pacing, pausing, and using correct word stress.

We also worked on softening his Dutch accent slightly, making small tweaks to his pronunciation for greater clarity and impact. Alongside that, we focused on being well-informed and prepared. We looked especially at answering key leadership questions, such as how to deal with underperformance or how to manage conflict. I also showed him how to glance into the camera when making an important point to create a sense of direct connection.

By the end of our work together, Barry came across as mature, confident, and professional. The transformation was like night and day. As a result, he got the promotion and is now thoroughly enjoying his new role. It was a real triumph for Barry — and, quietly, for me too.

Food for Thought

1. What's your goal right now?

→ *Are you preparing for a job interview, a promotion conversation, a Q&A session — or simply aiming to feel more at ease when speaking at work or amongst internationals?*

____

____

____

____

2. How do you feel about small talk?

→ *Do you enjoy it, avoid it, or simply not know what to say?*

→ *What topics feel natural — and which feel awkward or unfamiliar?*

____

____

____

____

3. How do you feel about answering questions on the spot?

→ *Does Q&A make you nervous, or do you see it as a chance to connect?*

→ *What kinds of questions would you love to feel more confident answering?*

4. What's your biggest concern — and where might it come from?

→ *Is it nerves, pronunciation, clarity, thinking under pressure — or something else?*

→ *When did you first start feeling unsure about this area? What might help you reframe it?*

5. A small intention for my next interview, Q&A or professional conversation:

→ *What mindset, phrase, or body language cue do you want to carry with you into that moment?*

A Few Final Words

You've now explored tools for finding your English voice, telling stories that connect, using your body with confidence, and speaking with clarity under pressure. Each skill is valuable, but they only truly thrive when paired with self-compassion.

All too often, we're harsher on ourselves than we would ever dream of being on anyone else. We become our own sternest critic, noticing every flaw, every hesitation, and every less-than-perfect moment. Our brains are wired to latch onto these imperfections — not because we're flawed, but because we've been trained that way.

From a young age, many of us grew up in systems that emphasised marks, rankings, and constant comparison. However well-intentioned, those systems leave deep grooves in our thinking. They make us feel that if we're not perfect from the start, we shouldn't even try. They push us to measure ourselves against others — and too often, we come up short. I've struggled with this in my role as a teacher, because I don't believe in comparing students. To me, every student is on their own unique path — just like you.

It's worth noting that there's a big difference between looking up to someone you admire and comparing yourself to them. One can be inspiring; the other can chip away at your confidence. Admiration can motivate you to grow, while comparison often leaves you feeling 'less than,' even when you're making real progress. And that's why it's important to remember what you already do so well.

As a non-native professional, you step into situations every day that would unsettle even the most confident native speaker. You join meetings, give presentations, answer questions, and take part in conversations in a language that isn't your first. You adapt to unfamiliar cultural cues. You share ideas, make decisions, and influence others — all outside your comfort zone. That's not just skill; that's courage.

Self-compassion means recognising this and giving yourself credit for showing up time and again. It's treating yourself with the same patience and encouragement you would offer a friend in your place. It's understanding that mistakes are not proof you don't belong — they're proof that you're learning.

And remember: every new day is an opportunity to take the next small step. Each one counts. Those steps, however modest they may feel, carry you forward, making you not only a stronger communicator but also a braver, kinder one. We're all works in progress, and that's the beauty of it. There's always room to grow, to connect, and to surprise ourselves. I'll leave you with a beautiful piece of wisdom I read many years ago:

Keep climbing the mountain, but pause now and then to enjoy the view.

Toolbox 1: Common Pronunciation Issues

Certain pronunciation challenges are more common depending on your first language. This Toolbox builds on the **three-step method** from Section 1.5 (Word → Sentence → Fluency) to help you target your most common tricky sounds. If your language isn't listed, choose the one most similar – the same method works for all. Of course, there are many more difficult sounds you will run into, but to not overwhelm you, I have only used the most common ones here.

How to Use This Toolbox

- Review the three-step method in Section 1.5. Then find your language below and follow the drills.
- Practise the words and sentences **slowly and clearly**, then build up to normal speed.
- Record yourself, listen back, and adjust for clarity. Try minding your intonation (stress patterns, inflection, and pitch) too.

Spanish

1. **Extra word practice**: value, visit, voice, berry, boat, very

   → To make the /v/ sound: Place your top teeth lightly on your bottom lip and let the sound vibrate as you use your voice. Think of a 'buzz' at the front of your mouth.

   → To make the /b/sound : Close your lips fully, then release a little burst of air as you use your voice. It's like starting a gentle 'pop' sound.

2. **Extra sentence practice**: Victor values a very big boat. / The berry is very sweet.

3. **Extra fluency practice**: *Victor visited the vineyard and valued the vintage wine. He said the very big barrels were beautiful to see.*

Dutch

1. **Extra word practice**: cab, rib, bag, sob, tab, bib

   → Finish the word with a clear, soft ending. Softening the last consonant will result in lengthening the vowel sound.

2. **Extra sentence practice**: The cab driver had a big bag. / Don't sob, grab the bib.

3. **Extra fluency practice**: *I grabbed the bag from the cab and paid the tab. Inside, there was a rib of beef and a bib for the baby. I gave the bib to Mum before heading to bed.*

French

1. **Extra word practice**: hat, hand, happy, think, thin, this, that
   → To make the /h/ sound: Open your mouth slightly and let out a gentle breath of air before the vowel. It's just warm air — no voice.
   → To make the /th/ sound (as in *think, thin*): Place your tongue lightly between your teeth and blow air out gently — no voice. The air should pass freely.
   → To make the /th/ sound (as in *this, that*): Place your tongue lightly between your teeth and blow air out gently **with your voice**. You should feel a gentle buzzing in your throat.

2. **Extra sentence practice**: He had a hat in his hand. / This thin cat is happy.

3. **Extra fluency practice**: *He had a headache and held his head in his hands. 'This thing will pass,' he thought, as he thanked his host for the hot tea.*

German

Use the three-step method with /w/ and /v/ contrast.

1. **Extra word practice**: wine, west, wave, very, vivid, vase

   → To make the /w/ sound: Round your lips into a small circle and push the sound forward, then relax into the vowel.

   → To make the /v/ sound: Place your top teeth lightly on your bottom lip and let the sound vibrate as you use your voice. Think of a 'buzz' at the front of your mouth.

2. **Extra sentence practice**: We went west with very vivid ideas. / The wave was very high.

3. **Extra fluency practice**: *We went west with very warm weather on our side. The vivid colours of the wildflowers waved in the wind.*

Italian

Use the three-step method with English diphthongs and varied vowel lengths. **A diphthong** is when you glide from one sound into another within the same syllable. <u>Example</u>: In *time* /taɪm/, you start with an 'ah' sound, then your mouth moves toward an 'ee' sound. In *go* /goʊ/, you start with 'oh' and glide toward 'oo.'

1. **Extra word practice**: go, phone, make, cake, time, smile

   → Start the vowel with your mouth in one position, then glide smoothly to a second position in the same sound — no pause in between.

2. **Extra sentence practice**: He made a joke on the phone at five. / I smiled at the time we met.

3. **Extra fluency practice**: *He made a cake and took it home. Later, he joked about the time it took, smiling as he poured the tea.*

Mandarin

Use the three-step method with /r/ vs /l/ distinction and English stress patterns.

1. **Extra word practice:** right, light, rice, lice, really, lily

   → To make the /r/ sound: Curl the tip of your tongue slightly upward without touching the roof of your mouth, and pull the sound back in your mouth.

   → To make the /l/ sound: Place the tip of your tongue just behind your top teeth and let the sound flow over the sides of your tongue.

2. **Extra sentence practice**: Lily really likes rice. / The light is on the right.

3. **Extra fluency practice**: *Lily likes to read in the light of the morning. She really enjoys rice for breakfast before running to work.*

Japanese

Use the three-step method with /r/ vs /l/ and final consonants.

1. **Extra word practice**: rock, lock, red, led, read, lid

   → To make the /r/ sound: Curl the tip of your tongue slightly upward without touching the roof of your mouth, and pull the sound back in your mouth.

   → To make the /l/ sound: Place the tip of your tongue just behind your top teeth and let the sound flow over the sides of your tongue.

2. **Extra sentence practice**: He read the red book on the rock. / She locked the lid.

3. **Extra fluency practice**: *He really liked the red lock on the box. Later, he read a letter and realised the lid was stuck.*

Remember: Always start slowly and exaggerate the target sound. Once you're confident, speed up to natural speech.

Toolbox 2: Take Your Mouth to the Gym

Some English sounds can feel awkward at first – especially if they don't exist in your native language. That's completely normal! The good news is, your mouth and brain can adapt with practice.

Think of these tongue twisters as mini workouts: they stretch, strengthen, and fine-tune the muscles you use for clear, confident English.

Remember: English is spoken mainly at the front of the mouth. Start slowly and focus on accuracy before speed. As it begins to feel more natural, gradually pick up the pace. Say each one out loud several times – and don't be afraid to laugh if you stumble.

Note: If you're not familiar with the phonetic alphabet, you can simply skip the symbols and follow the words.

Vowel Sounds:

/iː/ – as in *see, me, tree*

- Three green trees were seen by me.
- Please keep the bees away from me.
- He agreed to meet me at three.

/æ/ – as in *cat, hat, flat*

- Alice asked Alan to pass the apple.
- The fat cat sat on Matt's hat.
- Sally's backpack snapped at the back.

Consonant Sounds:

/v/ – as in *voice, very, vase*

- Vivian loves velvet vests.

- Vera viewed various vintage videos.
- A very valuable vase vanished.

/θ/ — as in *think, thirty, thank*

- Thirty-three thirsty thieves thought they'd thunder through Thursday.
- Think thin thoughts on Thursdays.
- The theatre theme thrilled Theo.

/ð/ — as in *this, those, brother*

- Those feathers are smoother than these.
- The other brother bothered their mother.
- This is the path that they'd rather not take.

Contrasting sounds: Sometimes it's helpful to practise pairs of sounds that are easy to mix up:

/v/ vs /f/

- Fred and Viv fought over five fat fish.
- Very funny, Fred — but five fish is far too few.

/s/ vs /ʃ/ — *see* vs *she*

- She sells sea shells by the seashore.
- Silly sheep should sleep soundly.

/l/ vs /r/

- Red lorries run regularly along rural roads.
- Larry rarely lets Lily read long letters.

Now try some longer tongue twisters (and have fun with them!):

- Vera's very vibrant voice vanished when she ventured to voice her views on virtual visibility.
  (Practises: /v/, /w/, rhythm and word stress)

- Thirty thoughtful thieves thanked Theo for thoroughly threading thirty-three thick threads.
  (Practises: /θ/, /ð/, /t/, clusters)

- Rita regularly runs red rural roads while reading riddles to restless rabbits.
  (Practises: /r/, /l/, /s/, rhythm)

- Should Sheila share her shiny shoes with shy Sean on Sunday's short show?
  (Practises: /ʃ/, /s/, sentence melody)

- Phil felt fearful on Friday, facing five fierce fitness fanatics flipping and flying.
  (Practises: /f/, /v/, and vowel rhythm)

- While Wendy was wondering where William went, Walter whispered wildly in the wind.
  (Practises: /w/, /r/, breath control)

- Lucy learned the lyrics late, loudly laughing and losing her lovely lilting lines.
  (Practises: /l/, vocal agility, stress timing)

- Bob brought bright blue balloons, but Billy burst both before breakfast.
  (Practises: /b/, /br/, /bl/, short vowels)

- Though they thought they'd thrive, those thorough theorists thoroughly tired themselves out.
  (Practises: /θ/, /ð/, rhythm & word endings)

- I rarely realise how regularly red robins rest on ragged railway railings.
  (Practises: /r/, /l/, natural rhythm and intonation)

Toolbox 3: Practising English Rhythm

As we saw in Chapter 1, English has a natural rhythm, with some words stressed and others gliding by more lightly. Getting a feel for this rhythm, together with using natural inflection in your voice, is one of the most effective ways to sound clearer, more confident, and much easier to follow.

Try reading the following sentences out loud. Focus on the stressed syllables and vary your pitch and tone to match the meaning. Let your voice fall at the end of a statement and rise on a question. Don't rush; go slowly, and let the rhythm guide you (just as when you listen to music!). Repeat a few times until it starts to feel more natural.

Everyday work and meetings:

- We need to FIN-ish this TO-*day.* ↘
- The MEET-ing is at TWO o'-*CLOCK.* ↘
- Let's FO-cus on the MAIN *task.* ↘
- Can you SEND me the re-PORT by to-MOR-row? ↗
- We'll have to POST-pone the PRO-ject until NEXT *week.* ↘

Professional communication:

- The CLI-ents are WAIT-ing for CLEAR com-mu-ni-CA-*tion.* ↘
- To im-PROVE our MAR-ket share, we'll need to a-DAPT to the LA-test *trends.* ↘
- The KEY to suc-CESS is in-no-VA-tion, not rep-e-TI-*tion.* ↘
- Let's BRAIN-storm some CRE-a-tive so-LU-tions for the SUPPLY chain DE-*lay.* ↘

Academic and study-related:

- The LI-brary is CLOSED on SUN-*days.* ↘
- Please sub-MIT your as-SIGN-ments on *TIME.* ↘
- I have a QUES-tion about the LEC-*ture.* ↘
- The RE-search FO-cuses on sus-TAIN-able de-VELOP-*ment.* ↘
- Can you ex-PLAIN the CON-cept more CLEAR-ly? ↗

Clarity and citation:

- It's im-POR-tant to CITE your SOUR-ces cor-RECT-*ly.* ↘
- The pro-POSED hy-POTH-e-sis does not FUL-ly ex-PLAIN the re-*SULTS.* ↘
- IN-ter-dis-ci-PLI-nary RE-search often re-QUIRES a BAL-ance of THEO-ry and PRAC-*tice.* ↘
- The PEER-re-VIEW PRO-cess guar-an-TEES the QUA-li-ty of ac-a-DEM-ic pub-li-CA-*tions.* ↘

Business and entrepreneurship:

- I have a NEW BIZ-ness i-*DE-a.* ↘
- The MAR-ket is GROW-ing RAP-id-*ly.* ↘
- We need to RAISE some CAP-i-*tal.* ↘
- START-ups must FO-cus on de-LIV-er-ing VAL-*ue.* ↘
- It's im-POR-tant to de-VE-lop a strong BRAND i-DEN-ti-*ty.* ↘

Investment and communication:

- The in-VEST-or's FEED-back was ex-TREM-ly HELP-*ful.* ↘

- To SCALE the BIZ-ness, we'll need to in-CREASE our ON-line PRE-*sence.* ↘
- EN-tre-pre-NEURS need to BAL-ance RISK and in-no-VA-*tion.* ↘
- Col-lab-o-RA-tion with PART-ners is es-SEN-tial for LONG-TERM SUCC-*ess.* ↘

Banking and finance:

- I'd like to O-pen a SAV-ings ac-*COUNT.* ↘
- What's the IN-trest RATE on this LOAN? ↗
- The BANK is CLOZD on PUB-lic HOL-i-*days.* ↘
- You need to pro-VIDE PROOF of IN-come for the ap-pli-CA-*tion.* ↘

Processes and systems:

- Can you ex-PLAIN how the MORT-gage PRO-cess WORKS? ↗
- The TRANS-ac-tion was SUC-cess-*ful.* ↘
- ON-line BANK-ing is more con-VEN-ient, but re-QUIRES STRONG-er se-CU-ri-ty MEAS-*ures.* ↘
- The GLO-bal fi-NAN-cial CRIS-is IM-pact-ed the BANK-ing SEC-tor sig-NIF-i-cant-*ly.* ↘
- To MAN-age RISKS, we need a com-pre-HEN-sive ap-PROACH to port-FO-lio di-VER-si-fi-CA-*tion.* ↘

Toolbox 4: Basic Presentation Framework

This toolbox is designed to help you create presentations that are clear, engaging, and easy to follow across languages and cultures.

Step 1: Plan with Clarity in Mind

a. **Audience profile**

- Professional background: What do they know already?
- Cultural diversity: Avoid humour, slang, or culture-specific references that may not translate.
- Language level: Short, clear sentences are easier to follow.

b. **Message discipline**

- Write your **main point** in one sentence: '*We can reduce delivery time by 20% using a new scheduling system.*'
- Everything in your presentation should connect to this point.

c. **Story selection**

Choose a story that is **work-relevant, universal, and relatable** (e.g., the frustration of deliveries arriving late, overcoming a project challenge, solving a client problem, improving a process).

Step 2: Build the International-Friendly Story Arc

Use a 5-part structure, which is easy to follow without advanced language skills:

1. **Context** – Where we are now

- Describe the setting simply: who, where, what.

- Use 2–3 short sentences: *'Our sales team tracks customer leads using spreadsheets. Each region keeps its own file, and updates are shared by email.'*

2. **Challenge** – What's wrong or could be improved

- State the problem directly: *'Our current system is slow and often causes delays. Our process is slow because updates are shared by email, leading to version confusion and delays. Teams waste time checking which file is correct.'*
- Use a simple visual if possible.

3. **Action** – What we did or propose to do

- Explain the steps in logical order. *'We introduced a single online CRM tool. We trained all sales reps on entering and updating leads. We set automatic reminders for follow-ups and reporting.'*
- Keep sentences short and verbs active. (*introduced, trained, set)*

4. **Result** – What happened or could happen

- Give clear outcomes: *'Delivery of reports is now 20% faster. Everyone sees the same data in real time.'*
- Show before/after contrast visually.

5. **Next step** – What you want from the audience

- Be specific: *'We need your approval to roll out the CRM to all regions.'*

Step 3: Slide & Language Guidelines for Multicultural Audiences: One Message Per Slide.

- Use **simple headings**: 'The Problem,' 'The Solution,' 'The Results.'

- **Limit text**: max 6–8 words per line, 3–4 lines per slide.
- **Avoid idioms**: say 'start' instead of 'kick off,' 'improve' instead of 'step up our game.'
- **Use internationally recognised visuals** (graphs, charts, icons).

Step 4: Storytelling Techniques That Work Cross-Culturally

- **Universal themes**: problem-solving, teamwork, innovation, overcoming challenges.
- **Numbers & visuals**: data is understood in any language.
- **Sequential markers**: '*First... Next... Finally...*' help listeners follow even if they miss some words.
- **Repetition for emphasis**: repeat your main point at least 3 times — in the intro, middle, and closing.
- **Clear transitions**: '*Now let's look at...*' or '*The next point is...*' help guide listeners.

Step 5: Example Flow (10-minute presentation)

- **Opening hook** – A relatable workplace challenge: '*Imagine waiting 3 days for a document you need urgently...*'
- **Context** – The current process.
- **Challenge** – The impact of slow delivery.
- **Action** – Your proposed solution.
- **Result** – Expected or actual measurable improvements.
- **Call to action (CTA)** – What you want them to do.
- **Closing** – Return to the opening image or story, now with a positive ending.

Toolbox 5: Storytelling Template

(Use with Toolbox 4, *Step 4: Storytelling Techniques)*

Goal: Fill in each section in simple, clear sentences (10–15 words max). Use bullet points if needed. Avoid slang and idioms.

Step 1 – Main Message

What is the single most important point you want people to remember?

- Main Message: ______________________________

Step 2 – Audience Check

Who will you present to? What do they care about?

- Role or department: _________________________
- Knowledge level on topic: _____________________
- Their main interest or concern: ________________

Step 3 – The 5-Part Story

- **Context** – Where we are now (who, where, what).
- **Challenge** – What's wrong or needs improvement (facts, examples, or personal/shared frustration).
- **Action** – What you did or propose to do (steps or changes).
- **Result** – What happened or will happen (clear, measurable outcomes).
- **Next Step** – What you want the audience to do (specific action).

Step 4 – Slide Outline

- **Title** – Main message

- **Hook** – Short personal story, frustration, or *'Imagine if…'* scenario
- **Context** – Current state
- **Challenge** – Problem and impact
- **Action** – Solution or plan
- **Result** – Benefits or improvements
- **Next Step** – Call to action
- **Closing** – Return to your opening story/example

Step 5 – Language Tips

- Keep sentences short and direct.
- Use active verbs (e.g., improve, reduce, achieve, build).
- Avoid culture-specific humour or idioms.
- Repeat your main message at the start, middle, and end.

Step 6 – Practice Prompts

Use these sentence starters to keep your story clear:

- *'Today I want to talk about…'*
- *'The problem we face is…'*
- *'Imagine if you were waiting…'*
- *'This matters because…'*
- *'We can solve this by…'*
- *'This will help us…'*
- *'The next step is…'*
- *'To summarise, remember that…'*

Toolbox 6: A Quick Vocab Booster for Everyday Conversations

Whether you're networking, making small talk at a conference, joining a team meeting, or just chatting with colleagues, these everyday expressions will help you sound confident and connected. As I mentioned in 5.4, many non-native speakers know the formal vocabulary of their field, but struggle with the casual, natural-sounding phrases that help build rapport. This toolbox is for that!

Starting a conversation:

- *'So, how's your week going?'*
- *'What did you do over the weekend?'*
- *'I've been meaning to ask you...'*
- *'By the way, I loved what you said in that meeting earlier.'*
- *'I saw your post online — really interesting!'*

Connecting with others:

- *'Same here.'*
- *'Tell me more about that.'*
- *'That makes total sense.'*
- *'I hadn't thought about it that way.'*
- *'You're absolutely right.'*
- *'Oh, I can relate to that!'*

Sounding fluent (without being too formal):

- *'Here's the thing...'*
- *'What I mean is...'*

- *'Let's dive in.'*
- *'Let me think for a second...'*
- *'That's a great point.'*
- *'Basically, what happened was...'*
- *'It's kind of like...'*
- *'Long story short...'*

Clarifying or keeping the conversation on track:

- *'Just to be clear...'*
- *'If I understand you correctly...'*
- *'Let me rephrase that.'*
- *'Let's come back to that in a moment.'*
- *'I'll circle back to that later.'*

Changing topic or ending naturally:

- *'Anyway, as I was saying...'*
- *'On a different note...'*
- *'That reminds me...'*
- *'Before I forget...'*
- *'Well, I'd better let you get on.'*
- *'Let's catch up again soon!'*

Tip: Listen for these phrases in meetings, podcasts or films and jot them down in a notebook or on your phone. You don't need to memorise them all, just pick a few and try them out until they start to feel natural.

Toolbox 7: Native Speaker Habits

Your aim here is not to morph into a native speaker, but it is to your advantage to adopt some native speaker habits – especially when you find yourself mingling with native speakers. I've included ones that make you easier to follow and easier to connect with.

Use Common, Flexible Words

Some words and expressions pop up in English all the time; they're natural, helpful, and easy to sprinkle into your speech. Try using words like the following to add rhythm, help you connect ideas, and make your speech feel more fluid and relaxed.

- *Actually*
- *I mean*
- *Basically*
- *Sort of / kind of*
- *Maybe*
- *Of course*
- *You know*
- *Well*
- *By the way*
- *To be honest*

Soften Your Questions with Tags

Non-native speakers often don't quite get the questions 'right,' and say things like: '*You've done this before, no*?' and '*This makes sense, yes*?' Instead, practise using question tags. Here are a few easy ones to practise:

- *'You've done this before, haven't you?'*
- *'It's quite a challenge, isn't it?'*
- *'You don't mind, do you?'*
- *'This makes sense, doesn't it?'*

Phrasal Verbs

One thing that can instantly make your speech sound more natural is the use of phrasal verbs — short **verb + particle** combinations like *give up, run into,* or *take off.* Native speakers use them all the time, especially in conversation.

I encourage clients to use phrasal verbs in presentations when speaking to a **native English audience**, as they bring clarity, relatability, and fluency. For example, instead of saying *Let's postpone the meeting,* a native speaker might say *Let's put off the meeting.* It sounds less formal and fits naturally in conversation.

Important note: With an **international audience**, be careful — phrasal verbs are often harder for non-native listeners to understand. Therefore, like idioms, they are sometimes best left out.

Phrasal Verbs to Try (with short, simple examples)

- **brush up** - improve or refresh knowledge/skills
  I need to brush up on my Spanish before my trip to Barcelona.

- **figure out** - solve or understand
  I finally figured out the answer to the problem.

- **run into** - meet by chance or encounter difficulties
  I ran into an old friend yesterday.
  We ran into difficulties during the project.

- **take off** - leave suddenly or become successful
  He took off without saying goodbye.
  Her business has really taken off this year.

- **give up** - stop trying
  I won't give up on my goals.

- **pick up** - collect or learn
  Can you pick up the kids from school?
  I always pick up new words when I read.

- **turn down** - reject
  I had to turn down the job offer.

- **bring up** - mention
  She brought up an interesting point in the meeting.

- **work out** - exercise or solve
  I work out at the gym every morning.
  We worked out a solution to the problem.

- **find out** - discover
  I just found out the meeting has been moved to Friday.

- **carry out** - perform or complete a task
  We need to carry out a full review before launching the product.

- **cut down on** - reduce
  We should cut down on unnecessary expenses this quarter.

- **go over** - review
  Let's go over the proposal one more time before sending it.

- **look into** - investigate or research
  We'll look into the cause of the delay and get back to you.

- **point out** - highlight or indicate
  She pointed out an error in the financial report.

- **put together** - assemble or create
  I'll put together a draft agenda for the meeting.

- **set up** - arrange or organise
  Let's set up a call with the client next week.

- **sort out** - organise or resolve
  We need to sort out the payment issue before the deadline.

- **turn up** - appear or arrive unexpectedly
  Only half the invited guests turned up.

- **come across** - find by chance or appear to others
  I came across an interesting article yesterday.
  She comes across as very confident in meetings.

- **get along (with)** - have a good relationship
  I get along well with my colleagues.

- **keep up with** - stay informed or maintain the same pace
  It's hard to keep up with all the industry changes.

Toolbox 8: Basic Pitch Template

The 'Value–Why–Proof–CTA' Flow

Share the Value (what's in it for them)

- Start with the problem you solve **and** the benefit they'll get.
- Keep it specific and measurable if possible.

  'Small retail stores lose an average of 12% in revenue due to stockouts. Our platform predicts demand with 95% accuracy, so they never miss a sale.'

Share Your Why (make it human)

- 2–3 sentences max.
- Show personal connection **that directly relates** to the problem.
- Use language that makes them feel you're deeply committed.

  'I grew up in a family-run store, and I saw firsthand how one missed shipment could wipe out a week's profits. That's why I built this solution — so small business owners can compete like the big guys.'

Back it Up with Proof (build credibility)

- Show results, traction, or credentials.
- Match proof style to audience: metrics for investors, testimonials for partners, awards for public audiences.

  'In the last 6 months, we've onboarded 120 retailers who've increased sales by an average of 14% using our system.'

Close with a Call to Action (guide the next step)

- Make it specific and easy to say yes to.

  'We're raising $250k to expand to 500 more stores by next year. Let's talk about how you can be part of that growth.'

Why this works:

- You connect emotionally with your why.
- You reassure your listeners with proof.
- You direct them to the next step.

In section 5.5, I mentioned that some audiences may not be particularly interested in your 'why,' and in those cases, you can leave it out altogether. But if you *do* want to include it, here's how to do so in a way that strengthens your pitch rather than distracting from it.

The examples below use the same **Value–Why–Proof–CTA** structure, but they're tailored for two different types of listeners. Notice how the 'why' shifts in emphasis and length depending on the audience — more prominent for a heart-driven group, shorter and more business-focused for a metrics-driven one. The key difference is:

- **Heart-driven pitch**: Puts human impact up front, with the 'why' adding emotional resonance.
- **Metrics-driven pitch**: Still includes the 'why,' but keeps it shorter and directly tied to business performance.

Heart-Driven Audience (Non-profit board, socially conscious investors, creative collaborators)

- **Value**: *'Workplace stress costs the global economy over $300 billion a year, but more importantly, it takes a huge toll on people's health and families. Our app gives employees daily mindfulness exercises and community support to help them thrive.'*

- **Why**: *'Five years ago, I burned out so badly I couldn't work for three months. I learned that small, consistent support can prevent big crises — and I wanted to make that accessible to everyone.'*
- **Proof**: *'Since launching, 82% of users report reduced stress within two weeks, and our longest pilot partner has seen a 30% drop in stress-related sick days.'*
- **CTA**: *'We're looking for partners who care about bringing mental wellness to every workplace — I'd love to explore how you could be part of this.'*

Metrics-Driven Audience (venture capital firm, procurement manager, corporate decision-maker)

- **Value**: *'Stress-related burnout costs companies an average of $3,400 per employee each year. Our app reduces absenteeism and improves retention through targeted daily wellness prompts.'*
- **Why**: *'I've experienced burnout firsthand, and I built this to make sure employees stay healthy — because healthy employees drive healthy companies.'*
- **Proof**: *'In our latest pilot, we cut stress-related sick days by 30% and improved retention by 18%, generating an ROI of 4.2x in the first year.'*
- **CTA**: *'We're onboarding new enterprise clients this quarter — I'd be happy to show you the full ROI breakdown for your team.'*

Toolbox 9: Troubleshooting Common Speaking Situations

Even with good preparation, things don't always go smoothly — and that's completely normal. Thankfully, many challenges can be anticipated and gently worked around. Below are a few common situations you might run into, and how to handle them with confidence and grace.

You forget a word mid-sentence

It happens to everyone — even native speakers! Instead of freezing, try one of these:

- *'Sorry, the word's escaping me — what I mean is...'*
- *'Let me rephrase that...'*
- *'In other words...'*

Often, your brain catches up while you're bridging the gap. Keep going — you're allowed to pause and regroup.

Someone speaks too quickly or unclearly

You don't need to nod and pretend. Try:

- *'Could you please repeat that a bit more slowly?'*
- *'I didn't quite catch that — do you mind saying it again?'*

Asking for clarity is professional. It shows you're engaged and taking the conversation seriously.

You're asked a question you didn't understand

Take a breath and stay calm. You can say:

- *'Just to be sure I understand — are you asking about...?'*

- *'That's a good question. Could you explain what you mean by...?'*

Asking for clarification gives you time to think and helps ensure you give a relevant answer.

You start rambling and lose your thread

This happens easily when nerves take over. Try this reset:

- *'Let me start that again more clearly.'*
- *'What I want to say is this...'*
- *'To sum up...'*

Short, grounding phrases like these help you refocus — and your audience will appreciate the clarity.

Someone uses idioms or cultural references you don't know

This happens all the time! You can always ask:

- *'I'm not sure I know that phrase — could you explain it?'*
- *'That expression's new to me — what does it mean?'*

Native speakers often use idioms without realising, and they'll likely be happy to explain.

You're translating from your own language

If you're still forming sentences in your head first, try to think in shorter, clearer phrases. Start by preparing a few of these ahead of time:

- *'The key point is...'*
- *'Here's what I'd suggest...'*
- *'In my experience...'*

Over time, your thinking and speaking will begin to line up more naturally.

You feel awkward during small talk

Remember, small talk isn't about trying to impress, it's about connection. Have a few go-to topics ready:

- Something light in the news
- An interesting place you visited
- An interesting article you read
- Your surroundings (e.g. '*I love this building — have you worked here long?*'). This way you also turn the conversation to the other person; it takes the pressure off and shows interest.

No matter what happens, don't beat yourself up. None of these moments define your ability or your worth as a human. Troubleshooting is not failure; it's exactly what confident, flexible speakers do.

Toolbox 10: Being Mindful of Different Cultural Norms

Why It Matters

When presenting to an audience from different cultural backgrounds, your style, pacing, and interaction may be interpreted in unexpected ways. A joke that works in one culture might confuse or offend in another. Silence could mean disagreement in one place, but careful consideration in another.

This toolbox gives you two things:

1. **Universal guidelines** to make your presentation clear, respectful, and engaging for any international audience.
2. **Regional snapshots** with quick tips on common presentation norms in different parts of the world, so you can adapt when needed.

Before we dive in, just a quick note on high- and low-context communication, a concept that comes from Edward T. Hall's communication theory:

- In **high-context cultures** (e.g., much of the Middle East, East Asia, parts of Africa and Latin America), much of the message is conveyed through tone, body language, shared history, and what is *not* said. People rely heavily on relationships and context to interpret meaning, and messages are often indirect.

- In **low-context cultures** (e.g., US, Canada, the Netherlands, Germany, Scandinavia), most of the message is in the words themselves. Communication is more direct, explicit, and task-focused, with less reliance on shared background knowledge.

When presenting, it helps to **blend both styles** — be clear and explicit for low-context listeners, but also provide background, stories, and relationship-building for high-context listeners.

1. Universal Guidelines for Any International Audience

Use these as your default 'safe mode' when you're unsure of your audience's background:

Focus on clarity above all

- Avoid idioms, slang, or overly complex language.
- Speak slowly, pause between key points, and define acronyms or technical terms.

Be culturally neutral but respectful

- Avoid jokes, metaphors, or visuals with strong regional, political, or religious connotations.
- Be mindful of gestures — as, for example, I mentioned in 3.4, the 'thumbs-up' can be offensive in some cultures.

Structure for all thinking styles

- Start with a clear summary or objective (for direct, low-context communicators).
- Follow with supporting context or stories (for high-context cultures).

Design inclusive slides

- Use visuals and diagrams for universal understanding.
- Avoid clutter; keep fonts large and legible.
- Use international date/number formats where possible.

Respect audience norms

- Some audiences may interrupt with questions; others will stay silent.

- Offer multiple ways to engage: 'Feel free to ask now' and 'You can also message me privately afterward.'

Be flexible with timing

- Western cultures tend to keep to schedule.
- Other cultures may prioritise relationship-building over strict timing.
- Plan buffer time for small talk or extended discussion.

Check for understanding

- Ask: 'Does that make sense?' or 'Would you like me to explain that differently?'
- Use quick polls or hand signals in virtual settings.

Use inclusive body language and voice

- Maintain open, friendly expressions.
- Avoid pointing directly; use open-handed gestures.
- Speak with a calm, confident tone — not overly aggressive or too soft.

Prepare for multicultural Q&A

- Be patient with silence; allow time for thought.
- Rephrase questions if needed.
- Offer follow-up after the presentation.

Know your audience ahead of time

- Ask organisers about nationalities, roles, and expectations.
- 'Are there any cultural considerations I should be aware of?' is a great pre-event question.

2. Regional Snapshots

(These are general tendencies — individuals will vary.)

Middle East

- High formality, strong respect for hierarchy and titles
- Indirect communication; public disagreement avoided.
- Relationship-building before business is valued.
- Visuals should be polished and culturally aware.
- Flexible time management — be patient with delays or extended introductions.

East Asia (e.g., Japan, China, Korea)

- Politeness, humility, and group harmony valued.
- Public questioning may be rare; follow up privately.
- Silence often signals thoughtfulness, not disinterest.
- Indirect communication but detailed explanations appreciated.

Northern Europe (e.g., Germany, Scandinavia)

- Direct, low-context communication; punctuality valued.
- Clear structure and evidence-based arguments are persuasive.
- Humour is fine but keep it subtle and professional.

Latin America

- Warm, personal introductions are common before business.
- Flexible timing; meetings may start late or run long.
- Storytelling and emotional connection resonate.
- Building rapport is key to persuasion.

North America (e.g., US, Canada)

- Relatively informal and direct style.
- Audiences expect clear 'what's in it for me' messaging.
- Interactive elements (polls, questions, stories) are well received.

Toolbox 11: Presentation Quick-Check

Whether it's for a meeting, a conference, or a webinar, this quick-check list will help you feel more confident, in control, and ready to engage your audience. Tick off what you've done — and spot what still needs your attention.

Message and Content:

- I've clarified my key message: what's the one thing I want my audience to remember?
- My content flows logically: beginning, middle, end.
- I've added examples or a personal story to make it more engaging.
- I've cut out any unnecessary jargon and kept language simple.
- I've thought about what my audience might *not* understand right away.

Text Preparation:

- I've written out my text (at least once) word-for-word.
- I've marked my script:
  - I've marked pauses.
  - I've underlined key words for emphasis.
- I've practised sentence stress and rhythm.
- I've practised out loud — as many times as possible!
- I sound like myself, not like I'm reading.

Slides & Visuals:

- My slides are clean, clear, and not overcrowded. One idea per slide (if possible).

- I've avoided long sentences and bullet points and used keywords and complementary images instead.**
- I've checked for spelling/grammar errors.
- Images or graphs support (not distract from) my story.
- Font size is large enough, even from the back of a room.

Language & Pronunciation:

- I've practised any difficult words or technical terms.
- I've checked word stress and intonation on key sentences.
- I've used Toolbox 3 or 4 to warm up (yes, take your mouth the gym!).
- I've listened to myself speak on a recording, or practised with a trusted friend or coach.

Body Language & Voice:

- I've rehearsed standing up and using hand gestures.
- I've practised speaking at a calm pace (not rushing!).
- I've checked that I'm **not** speaking in a flat tone; my voice has some life in it.
- I've practised breathing low and relaxing my shoulders.
- I've reminded myself to glance at the audience or into the camera (online!).

Mindset & Confidence:

- I've reminded myself why I said yes to this talk.
- I've visualised connecting with the audience.
- I've done something calming (or fun!) beforehand.
- I've prepared a few phrases to use if I forget something.
- I've reminded myself: I'm prepared. I'm perfectly safe.

Q&A Prep:

- I've thought about the most likely questions I might get.
- I've practised a few confident, simple responses.
- I've prepared a question or two to ask the audience if needed.

** I've often seen slides that are completely overloaded with text. This leaves the audience scrambling to read everything before the next one appears, all while trying to listen to the speaker. It's exhausting, and frankly, a sure way to lose your audience.

You'll notice that I advise you to leave out, or at least greatly reduce, bullet points on your slides. The reason is because lists of bullet points on slides are often dull and can cause your audience to switch off (I agree with speaker coach Andy Harrington, who amusingly talks of 'death by bullet point').

Bullet points also carry the risk of you simply repeating what's written on the slide word for word. Remember: **Your slides should complement your message, not compete with it**. One powerful image, a key word, or a thought-provoking quote can often do far more than a crowded list. In other words: less is more!

A Word of Thanks

I'm deeply grateful to the many inspirational people who've taught and supported me over the years — teachers, students, clients, colleagues, and friends. I would especially like to thank Yvonne de Jong, Arthur de Jong, Jan van Mersbergen, Aleid Fokkema, Hilary Dyer, Rachel Mathieson, and of course Martijn van den Heuvel for their invaluable encouragement and feedback on various projects throughout my studies and career.

I am also indebted to the many books that have informed, inspired, and accompanied me on my journey toward finding my voice and footing in the world. Some are practical, some moving or humorous, others quietly wise. In the bibliography are a few that have most influenced my work with clients and students — and, in turn, this book.

Note: I didn't use his course, but I've noticed that parts of my approach overlap with Peter Novak's *LinkedIn Learning* materials. I take it as a happy coincidence — and a reminder that good teaching often leads to similar ideas.

Select Bibliography

Ashton, Helen, and Sarah Shepherd. *Work on Your Accent: Clearer Pronunciation for Better Communication*. HarperCollins Publishers, 2020.

Berkun, Scott. *Confessions of a Public Speaker*. O'Reilly Media, Inc., 2010.

Brown, Brené. *The Gifts of Imperfection: Let Go of Who You Think You're Supposed to Be and Embrace Who You Are*. Gotham Books, 2016.

Carlson, Richard. *Don't Sweat the Small Stuff... and It's All Small Stuff*. Hyperion, 1997.

Carnegie, Dale. *The Art of Public Speaking*. Waking Lion Press, 2011.

Esposito, Janet. *In the Spotlight: Overcome Your Fear of Public Speaking and Performing*. Strong Books, 2001.

Gallo, Carmine. *Talk Like TED: The 9 Public Speaking Secrets of the World's Top Minds*. MacMillan Publishers, 2014.

Greene, Robert. *Mastery*. Profile Books Limited, 2012.

Hall, Kindra. *Stories That Stick: How Storytelling Can Captivate Customers, Influence Audiences, and Transform Your Business*. HarperCollins, 2019.

Jeffers, Susan. *Feel the Fear and Do It Anyway*. Vermilion, 2007.

McDonagh, Barry. *Dare: The New Way to End Anxiety and Stop Panic Attacks*. BMD Publishing, 2015.

Reynolds, Garr. *Presentation Zen: Simple Ideas on Presentation Design and Delivery*. New Riders, 2008

Printed in Great Britain
by Amazon

f39af0fe-fb3c-475b-b674-480519647a4eR01